Betty Crocker's

RED SPOON COLLECTION™

BEST RECIPES FOR

WEEKEND

BREAKFASTS

PRENTICE HALL

New York   London   Toronto   Sydney   Tokyo   Singapore

PRENTICE HALL GENERAL REFERENCE
15 Columbus Circle
New York, New York 10023

Copyright © 1991 by General Mills, Inc.,
Minneapolis, Minnesota

Published simultaneously in Canada by Prentice Hall Canada Inc.

PRENTICE HALL and colophons are registered
trademarks of Simon & Schuster, Inc.

BETTY CROCKER is a registered trademark
of General Mills, Inc.

RED SPOON COLLECTION is a trademark of General Mills, Inc.

Library of Congress Cataloging-in-Publication Data

Best recipes for weekend breakfasts.
    p.   cm.—(Betty Crocker's red spoon collection)
  Includes index.
  ISBN 0-13-068339-6
  1. Breakfasts. I. Series.
  TX733.B48 1991
  641.5'2—dc20
                                                    90-39877
                                                      CIP

Manufactured in the United States of America

10   9   8   7   6   5   4   3   2

First Edition

Front Cover: Belgian Waffles (page 84)

CONTENTS

INTRODUCTION

Everyone knows that breakfast is the most important meal of the day, the meal that literally "breaks the fast" imposed on our bodies as we sleep. If you finish dinner at 7 P.M. and wake up at 7 A.M., that's half a day your body has gone without food. It's no wonder that people who skip breakfast tend to be sluggish, have difficulty concentrating and in general have a harder time performing all mental and physical tasks.

Breaking Down the Breakfast Barrier

If everyone knows how crucial breakfast is for high performance, why is it so hard to get people to eat breakfast? It's a combination of factors and habits that can all be modified so that eating breakfast becomes a natural part of your everyday routine. Some people are simply bored with the same breakfast every day, while others think they can't digest anything but coffee in the morning. People who use great imagination in planning lunch and dinner forget to put that same energy into planning breakfast, and those who wouldn't dream of skipping lunch will pass up breakfast without a thought and then wonder why

they have a midmorning energy slump. But breakfast can be creative, satisfying and quick.

You can turn to the Red Spoon Tips (pages 97–108) in the back of this book to find answers to almost any breakfast problem—from suggestions for breakfasts that are nutritious yet different, and suggestions for tempting the appetite of non-breakfast eaters, to suggestions for express breakfasts that will have you well fed and out the door in about the same amount of time it takes to shower.

TGIF

With the busy schedules most people keep during the week, the weekend is the time to relax and enjoy entertaining friends, or to spend unhurried time with your family. With the recipes collected here, you will be able to indulge your appreciation of breakfast to the fullest, whether you want to savor old favorites such as waffles and French toast, or try new dishes. Gathered here are the answers to your weekend breakfast questions, from "What do I serve to a large crowd before a ski trip?" to "What's new for an easy, low-key breakfast for two?"

Breakfast Basics and Beyond

This breakfast cookbook will serve your needs, even when it's not the weekend. In Red Spoon Tips you will find all you need to know about the ever-popular egg, from how to buy and store eggs properly to how to cook them perfectly. Learn how to fry, scramble, soft-cook, hard-cook, poach and bake eggs the Betty Crocker way for perfect results every time. You will also find a section on how to brew coffee and tea exactly right, whether it's one cup in the morning or enough to serve a large group. You can check the simple chart included to see how long to reheat muffins, coffee cakes and biscuits in the microwave, whether they are frozen or at room temperature. With these guidelines, you'll be able to make a delicious, basic breakfast, as well as use the information as a springboard for more elaborate recipes.

Breakfast Bonanza

Within each chapter you will find ideas for entrées, beverages, breads and condiments that you can mix and match to serve your needs and fill the bill for any occasion. Looking for breakfast to serve just the two of you? Turn to Breakfast for Two chapter and try Western Omelets (page 7) with Four-Cheese and Scallion Muffins (page 17) and Chocolate-laced Kiwifruit with Orange Sauce (page 16), served with coffee. If you are looking for a hearty breakfast the whole family can linger over, browse through the Family Breakfasts chapter. Applesauce Pancakes (page 23) served with Spicy Cider Syrup (page 35), bacon and Honey Bee Ambrosia (page 31), will keep your family around the table and conversation humming.

When you're elected host for a breakfast event, don't panic. The Breakfast for a Crowd chapter will give you plenty of help, from Seafood Crepes (page 44) to Oven Scrambled Eggs (page 41). The Lazy Day Breakfasts chapter is for mornings when you want a delicious breakfast with a minimum of fuss. Whether you try Overnight Cinnamon Rolls (page 76), Quick Chili-Cheese Puff (page 67) or Oven Bacon (page 70), you're sure to have both the benefits of easy cooking and great taste.

Also explored in this breakfast roundup are recipes for holiday breakfasts that will give you welcome suggestions for impressive meals. Recipes for a special Holiday Braid (page 94) or Easy Valentine Strudels (page 91) may even inspire you to start a few new holiday traditions.

Wake Up and Smell the Coffee

Weekend breakfasts combine easy cooking with relaxed entertaining. It is a perfect way to see friends in an informal setting, without worrying about when the get-together will have to end. When you meet for breakfast, the conversation and camaraderie can flow into the afternoon. Be sure to have plenty of beverages on hand so you can relax and enjoy your guests, and let the day take its course. And however you wish to cook you'll be sure to find all the recipes you need right here.

· 1 ·
BREAKFAST FOR TWO

Western Omelets

6 eggs
½ cup finely chopped fully cooked smoked ham
1 small onion, chopped (about ¼ cup)
¼ cup chopped green bell pepper
2 tablespoons margarine or butter

Mix 3 eggs with fork just until whites and yolks are blended; stir in half of the ham, onion and bell pepper. Heat 1 tablespoon margarine or butter in 8-inch skillet or omelet pan over medium-high heat just until margarine begins to brown. As margarine melts, tilt skillet to coat bottom completely.

Quickly pour egg mixture, all at once, into skillet. Slide skillet back and forth rapidly over heat and, at the same time, stir quickly with fork to spread eggs continuously over bottom of skillet as they thicken. Let stand over heat a few seconds to lightly brown bottom of omelet.

Tilt skillet; run fork under edge of omelet, then jerk skillet sharply to loosen eggs from bottom of skillet. Fold portion of omelet nearest you just to center. (Allow for portion of omelet to slide up side of skillet.)

Grasp skillet handle; turn omelet onto warm plate, flipping folded portion of omelet over so far side is on bottom. Tuck sides of omelet under if necessary. Repeat with remaining ingredients.

Following pages: Western Omelets and Potato Wedges (page 13)

Scrambled Eggs with Peppers and Tomatoes

2 SERVINGS

1 medium green bell pepper, sliced
1 small onion, sliced
1 clove garlic, chopped
1/8 teaspoon salt
1/4 teaspoon dried thyme leaves
1 tablespoon plus 1 1/2 teaspoons olive oil
  or margarine
1 medium tomato, coarsely chopped
4 eggs
1/4 cup milk
1/4 cup 1/4-inch strips fully cooked smoked
  ham
1/4 teaspoon salt
1/8 teaspoon pepper

Cook and stir green peppers, onion, garlic, 1/8 teaspoon salt and the thyme in 2 teaspoons of the oil in 10-inch skillet over medium heat until green peppers are crisp-tender, about 8 minutes. Add tomatoes; heat until hot, about 2 minutes. Drain excess liquid from vegetables; place vegetables on platter. Keep warm.

Heat remaining oil in same skillet over medium heat until hot. Mix remaining ingredients; pour into skillet. Cook uncovered over low heat, stirring frequently, until eggs are thickened throughout but still moist, 3 to 5 minutes. Mound scrambled eggs in center of vegetables. Sprinkle with snipped parsley, if desired.

Eggs in Toast Cups

2 SERVINGS

2 slices whole wheat bread
4 teaspoons margarine or butter, softened
1/4 cup shredded Cheddar cheese (about
  1 ounce)
1 green onion (with tops), sliced
Dried marjoram leaves
4 eggs
2 teaspoons milk
Salt
Pepper
1 tablespoon toasted sliced almonds

Heat oven to 350°. Spread 1 side of each slice of bread with margarine. Press each slice, margarine side down, in 10-ounce individual casserole or custard cup. Divide cheese and onions among casseroles; sprinkle each with marjoram. Break 2 eggs into each casserole. Pour 1 teaspoon milk over each egg; sprinkle with salt, pepper and almonds. Place casseroles in jelly roll pan, 15 1/2 × 10 1/2 × 1 inch. Cook uncovered in oven until egg whites are set, 20 to 25 minutes.

Blue Cheese Soufflé

2 tablespoons dry bread crumbs
1/4 cup margarine or butter
1/4 cup all-purpose flour
1/8 teaspoon pepper
1/2 cup milk
1/2 cup dry white wine
1/2 package (4-ounce size) blue cheese,
    crumbled (about 1/2 cup)
3 eggs, separated
1/4 teaspoon cream of tartar
1/2 cup dairy sour cream
1/4 cup whipping cream

Heat oven to 350°. Butter 1-quart soufflé dish or casserole. Make a 4-inch-wide band of triple-thickness aluminum foil 2 inches longer than circumference of dish; butter 1 side of foil. Secure foil band, buttered side in, around outside edge of dish and sprinkle evenly with bread crumbs.

Heat margarine in 2-quart saucepan over low heat until melted. Stir in flour and pepper. Cook over low heat, stirring constantly, until smooth and bubbly; remove from heat. Stir in milk until blended; stir in wine. Heat to boiling, stirring constantly. Boil and stir 1 minute. Stir in cheese until melted; remove from heat.

Beat egg whites and cream of tartar in medium bowl on high speed until stiff but not dry. Beat egg yolks in small bowl on high speed until very thick and lemon colored, about 3 minutes; stir into cheese mixture. Stir about one-fourth of the beaten egg whites into cheese mixture. Fold cheese mixture into remaining egg whites.

Carefully pour into soufflé dish. Bake uncovered until knife inserted halfway between center and edge comes out clean, 50 to 60 minutes. Mix sour cream and whipping cream. Carefully remove foil band, and divide soufflé into portions, using 2 forks. Serve immediately with sour cream mixture. Sprinkle with chopped tomato and avocado or chopped apples and toasted almonds, if desired.

Ham Quiche

Cornmeal Quiche Shells (below)
1/3 cup shredded mozzarella cheese
2 tablespoons finely chopped fully cooked smoked ham
1 tablespoon finely chopped green onion (with top)
2 eggs
1/3 cup milk
1/4 teaspoon salt
6 drops red pepper sauce

Heat oven to 425°. Prepare Cornmeal Quiche Shells. Sprinkle cheese, ham and onion in shells. Beat remaining ingredients with fork in small bowl. Pour into shells. Bake uncovered 10 minutes. Reduce oven temperature to 300°. Bake 20 to 25 minutes or until knife inserted halfway between center and edge comes out clean.

CORNMEAL QUICHE SHELLS

1/3 cup all-purpose flour
1 tablespoon plus 1 teaspoon cornmeal
1/8 teaspoon salt
1 tablespoon plus 2 teaspoons shortening
5 to 6 teaspoons water

Mix flour, cornmeal and salt; cut in shortening thoroughly. Sprinkle in water, tossing with fork until all flour is moistened and pastry cleans side of bowl. Gather pastry into a ball. Divide into halves. Press each half firmly against bottom and side of two 8-ounce quiche dishes or 10-ounce custard cups.

Fresh Fruit and Cheese Platter

1 pear
1 apple
1 cup red and green seedless grapes
1 cup 2 ounces Swiss cheese
2 ounces Cheddar cheese
2 ounces Edam cheese

Slice fruit or leave whole. Arrange on platter with slices or wedges of cheese.

Easy Fruit Salad

½ *can (11-ounce size) mandarin orange*
segments
1 small banana, sliced
1 small apple, sliced
¼ *cup chopped dates*
Salad greens

Arrange fruits on greens; top with yogurt, if desired.

Potato Wedges

2 SERVINGS

2 medium potatoes, cut lengthwise into
eighths
Vegetable oil
Seasoned salt

Place potato wedges on rack in broiler pan. Brush with oil; sprinkle with seasoned salt. Set oven control to broil and/or 550°. Broil with tops about 3 inches from heat until brown, about 5 minutes. Turn; brush with oil. Sprinkle with seasoned salt. Broil until brown and fork-tender, about 5 minutes.

Maple-glazed Bacon

2 SERVINGS

½ *pound Canadian-style bacon, cut into*
¼*-inch slices*
2 tablespoons maple-flavored syrup

Heat oven to 325°. In ungreased small shallow baking dish, overlap bacon slices slightly. Drizzle syrup on slices. Bake uncovered until bacon is hot, about 35 minutes.

Following pages: Ham Quiche

Chocolate-laced Kiwifruit with Orange Sauce

2 SERVINGS

¼ cup plain yogurt
1½ teaspoons partially thawed frozen
  unsweetened orange juice concentrate
2 large kiwifruit, pared and cut into
  ¼-inch slices
1 tablespoon semisweet chocolate chips
½ teaspoon shortening

Mix yogurt and orange juice concentrate; spoon 2 tablespoons onto each of 2 dessert plates. Arrange 1 sliced kiwifruit over yogurt mixture on each plate. Heat chocolate chips and shortening over low heat, stirring constantly, until chocolate is melted. Carefully drizzle chocolate in thin lines over kiwifruit.

Harvest Celebration Cups

2 SERVINGS

1 cup cut-up fresh fruit
½ cup chilled sparkling pink Catawba
  grape juice

Divide fruit between 2 serving cups. Pour ¼ cup grape juice into each cup; stir once. Serve immediately.

Honey Strawberries

2 SERVINGS

1 tablespoon plus 1 teaspoon honey
2 teaspoons lime juice
2 cups sliced strawberries
Whipped topping

Mix honey and lime juice; gently stir in strawberries. Top with whipped topping.

Southwest Smoothie

2 SERVINGS

½ cup sliced banana
½ cup chopped mango, papaya or guava
2 cups milk
1 tablespoon honey

Place all ingredients in food processor workbowl fitted with steel blade or in blender container; cover and process on high speed until smooth. Strain if using mango.

Four-Cheese and Scallion Muffins

4 MUFFINS

1 egg
1¼ cups milk
¼ cup margarine or butter, melted
2 cups all-purpose flour
¼ cup chopped scallions (with tops)
¼ cup shredded mozzarella cheese
¼ cup shredded Romano cheese
¼ cup shredded Parmesan cheese
2 tablespoons finely chopped Bel Paese
   cheese
3 teaspoons baking powder
¼ teaspoon white pepper

Heat oven to 400°. Grease four 6-ounce custard cups. Beat egg in large bowl; stir in milk and margarine. Stir in remaining ingredients just until flour is moistened. Divide batter among cups (cups will be full). Place on cookie sheet.

Bake until golden brown, about 35 minutes. Immediately remove from cups.

Prosciutto and Sun-dried Tomato Muffins

4 MUFFINS

1 egg
1 cup milk
¼ cup vegetable oil
2 cups all-purpose flour
¾ cup finely chopped prosciutto (about
   ¼ pound)
½ cup chopped sun-dried tomatoes in
   olive oil, rinsed and drained
2 tablespoons snipped fresh basil
2½ teaspoons baking powder

Heat oven to 400°. Grease four 6-ounce custard cups. Beat egg in large bowl; stir in milk and oil. Stir in remaining ingredients just until flour is moistened. Divide batter among cups (cups will be full). Place on cookie sheet.

Bake until golden brown, about 35 minutes. Immediately remove from cups.

Whipped Honey-Orange Butter

1 CUP SPREAD

1 cup margarine or butter, softened
2 tablespoons honey
2 teaspoons grated orange peel

Beat margarine, honey and orange peel on medium speed until fluffy. Serve with bagels, if desired.

Following pages: Fresh Fruit and Cheese Platter, right (page 12) and Bagels with Whipped Honey-Orange Butter

Curried Spread

1 package (8 ounces) cream cheese,
*   softened*
2 teaspoons sugar
2 teaspoons curry powder
Dash of salt

Beat all ingredients until smooth. Serve with raisin toast, if desired.

Mocha Espresso

2 tablespoons instant cocoa mix
1 tablespoon plus 1 teaspoon instant
*   espresso coffee*
2 cups hot milk

Stir 1 tablespoon cocoa mix and 2 teaspoons espresso coffee (dry) into each cup of hot milk. Top with whipped cream and sprinkle with ground cinnamon, if desired.

· 2 ·

FAMILY BREAKFASTS

Home-style Scrambled Eggs

4 SERVINGS

4 eggs
3 tablespoons water
¾ teaspoon salt
¼ cup margarine or butter
1 medium cooked potato, cubed (about 1 cup)
3 tablespoons finely chopped onion
1 small zucchini, halved and sliced
1 tomato, chopped

Beat eggs, water and salt with fork. Heat margarine in 10-inch skillet over medium heat until melted; cook and stir vegetables in margarine 2 minutes. Pour egg mixture into skillet.

As mixture begins to set at bottom and side, gently lift cooked portions with spatula so that thin, uncooked portion can flow to bottom. Avoid constant stirring. Cook until eggs are thickened throughout but still moist, 3 to 5 minutes.

TO MICROWAVE: Omit margarine. Beat eggs, water and salt with fork in 1½-quart microwavable casserole. Stir in potato, onion and zucchini. Cover tightly and microwave on high, stirring every minute, until eggs are puffy and set but still moist, 4 to 5 minutes. (Eggs will continue to cook while standing.) Stir in tomato.

Broccoli and Swiss Cheese Frittata

6 SERVINGS

1 medium onion, chopped (about
    1/2 cup)
2 cloves garlic, finely chopped
2 tablespoons margarine or butter
1 tablespoon olive or vegetable oil
1 package (10 ounces) frozen chopped
    broccoli, thawed and drained
8 eggs
1/2 teaspoon salt
1/4 teaspoon pepper
1 cup shredded Swiss cheese (4 ounces)
1 to 2 tablespoons snipped fresh
    oregano leaves or 1 teaspoon dried
    oregano leaves
2 tablespoons shredded Swiss cheese

Cook onion and garlic in margarine and oil in 10-inch ovenproof skillet over medium heat, stirring frequently, until onion is tender, about 5 minutes. Remove from heat; stir in broccoli.

Beat eggs, salt and pepper until blended; stir in 1 cup cheese and the oregano. Pour over broccoli mixture. Cover and cook over medium-low heat until eggs are set around edge and light brown on bottom, 9 to 11 minutes.

Set oven control to broil. Broil frittata with top about 5 inches from heat until golden brown, about 2 minutes. Sprinkle with 2 tablespoons cheese; cut into wedges.

Crisp Waffles

3 10-INCH WAFFLES

2 eggs
1 3/4 cups milk
1/2 cup margarine or butter, melted, or
    salad oil
2 cups all-purpose* or unbleached flour
4 teaspoons baking powder
1 tablespoon sugar
1/2 teaspoon salt

Heat waffle iron. Beat eggs with hand beater until fluffy; beat in remaining ingredients just until smooth. Pour batter from cup or pitcher onto center of hot waffle iron. Bake until steaming stops, about 5 minutes. Remove waffle carefully.

BLUEBERRY WAFFLES: Sprinkle 2 to 4 tablespoons fresh or frozen blueberries (thawed and well drained) over batter immediately after pouring it onto the iron.

BRAN WAFFLES: Sprinkle 2 tablespoons whole bran cereal or bran flakes over batter immediately after pouring it onto the iron.

CHEESE AND BACON WAFFLES: Stir in 1 cup shredded sharp cheese (about 4 ounces). Arrange 4 short slices bacon, crisply fried, on batter immediately after pouring it onto the iron.

*If using self-rising flour, omit baking powder and salt.

Applesauce Pancakes

11 4-INCH PANCAKES

1 egg
1 cup all-purpose* or unbleached flour
½ cup milk
½ cup applesauce
¼ teaspoon ground cinnamon
2 tablespoons shortening, melted, or salad
*   oil*
1 tablespoon sugar
3 teaspoons baking powder
½ teaspoon salt

Beat egg with hand beater until fluffy; beat in remaining ingredients just until smooth. For thinner pancakes, stir in additional ¼ cup milk. Grease heated griddle if necessary. (To test griddle, sprinkle with few drops water. If bubbles skitter around, heat is just right.)

Pour about 3 tablespoons batter from tip of large spoon or from pitcher onto hot griddle. Cook pancakes until puffed and dry around edges. Turn and cook other sides until golden brown.

BUTTERMILK PANCAKES: Omit applesauce and cinnamon. Substitute 1 cup buttermilk for the milk. Decrease baking powder to 1 teaspoon and beat in ½ teaspoon baking soda.

CHEESE PANCAKES: Omit applesauce, cinnamon and sugar. Stir in 1 cup shredded Swiss or American cheese (about 4 ounces).

CORNMEAL PANCAKES: Omit applesauce and cinnamon. Substitute ½ cup cornmeal for ½ cup of the flour.

*If using self-rising flour, omit baking powder and salt.

Following pages: Broccoli and Swiss Cheese Frittata and Scones, right (page 53)

Blueberry Yogurt Pancakes

2 eggs
2 cups all-purpose flour
3 containers (6 ounces each) 100%
  natural blueberry yogurt
1/4 cup vegetable oil
2 tablespoons sugar
2 teaspoons baking powder
1 teaspoon baking soda
1/2 teaspoon salt

Beat eggs in medium bowl with hand beater until fluffy. Beat in remaining ingredients just until blended. Grease heated griddle if necessary. (To test griddle, sprinkle with few drops water. If bubbles skitter around, heat is just right.)

For each pancake, pour about 3 tablespoons batter from tip of large spoon or from pitcher onto hot griddle. Cook pancakes until puffed and dry around edges. Turn and cook other sides until golden brown.

Oatmeal Pancakes

2 egg whites
1 cup buttermilk
3/4 cup quick-cooking oats
1/2 cup all-purpose flour
1 tablespoon sugar
2 tablespoons vegetable oil
1 teaspoon baking powder
1/2 teaspoon baking soda

Beat egg whites in large bowl with hand beater until foamy. Stir in remaining ingredients. Grease heated griddle if necessary. (To test griddle, sprinkle with few drops water. If bubbles skitter around, heat is just right.)

For each pancake, pour about 3 tablespoons batter from tip of large spoon or from pitcher onto hot griddle. Cook pancakes until puffed and dry around edges. Turn and cook other sides until golden brown.

Oven French Toast

4 SERVINGS

3 tablespoons margarine or butter, melted
1/3 cup orange juice
2 tablespoons honey
3 eggs
8 slices French bread, each 1 inch thick

Pour margarine in jelly roll pan, 15½ × 10½ × 1 inch. Beat orange juice, honey and eggs with hand beater until foamy. Dip bread into egg mixture; place in pans. Drizzle any remaining egg mixture over bread. Cover and refrigerate no longer than 24 hours.

Heat oven to 450°. Bake uncovered until bottoms are golden brown, about 10 minutes; turn bread. Bake until bottoms are golden brown, 6 to 8 minutes longer.

Grilled Peanut Butter and Banana

4 SANDWICHES

Peanut butter
8 slices English muffin bread
2 medium bananas
Margarine or butter, softened

Spread peanut butter over one side of 4 slices bread; slice bananas and arrange on top. Top with remaining bread; spread top slices with margarine.

Place sandwiches, margarine sides down, in skillet. Spread top slices with margarine. Cook uncovered over medium heat until bottoms are golden brown, about 4 minutes; turn. Cook until bottoms are golden brown and peanut butter is melted, 2 to 3 minutes longer.

GRILLED PEANUT BUTTER AND BANANA WITH BACON: Place cooked bacon slices on bananas before topping with remaining bread.

Following pages: Oven French Toast, left, and Crisp Waffles, right (page 22) with Mixed Berry Syrup (page 35)

Sausage-Cheese Biscuit Sandwiches

4 SANDWICHES

1/4 cup shortening
2 cups all-purpose flour*
3 teaspoons baking powder
1 teaspoon salt
3/4 cup milk
1/2 package (8 ounces) brown-and-serve
    sausage patties
4 slices process American cheese

Heat oven to 450°. Cut shortening into flour, baking powder and salt with pastry blender until mixture resembles fine crumbs. Stir in just enough milk so dough leaves side of bowl and rounds up into a ball. (Too much milk makes dough sticky; not enough makes biscuits dry.)

Turn dough onto ungreased cookie sheet. Pat dough into 6-inch square with floured hands. Cut into 3-inch squares, cutting completely through dough. Brush with margarine or butter, melted. Bake 15 to 20 minutes. Immediately remove from cookie sheet; cool 5 minutes. Gently pull biscuits apart.

Meanwhile, cook sausage patties as directed on package. Split biscuits; layer one sausage patty and one cheese slice between each biscuit half.

*If using self-rising flour, omit baking powder and salt.

Mixed Fruit Salad

4 SERVINGS

1 1/2 cups blueberries or strawberry halves
1 papaya or 1 small cantaloupe, cut up
2 kiwifruit, sliced
Honey Dressing (below)

Mix blueberries, papaya and kiwifruit; toss with Honey Dressing. Serve on salad greens and sprinkle with toasted almonds, if desired.

HONEY DRESSING

1/4 cup bottled red wine vinegar and oil
    dressing
1 tablespoon honey
1/4 teaspoon poppy seed

Shake dressing, honey and poppy seed in tightly covered container.

Melon and Ham Platter

¹/₂ cantaloupe
¹/₂ honeydew melon
12 thin slices smoked fully cooked ham
1 lemon, cut into wedges

Cut each melon half into 6 wedges; pare. Arrange melon wedges on platter. Roll up slices of ham; place around melon. Garnish with lemon wedges. Cover and refrigerate no longer than 4 hours.

Cantaloupe Salads

6 SERVINGS

2 small cantaloupe
1 cup sliced strawberries
1 cup seedless green grapes
Lettuce leaves
1 container (24 ounces) small curd
   cottage cheese

Pare each cantaloupe. Cut off about 1 inch from ends of each cantaloupe. Cut up end pieces; mix with strawberries and grapes. Remove seeds from cantaloupe. Cut each cantaloupe into 3 even rings. Place rings on lettuce leaves on each of 6 plates; cut each ring into 1-inch pieces, retaining shape of ring. Spoon mixed fruit onto each ring. Spoon cottage cheese on each salad.

Honey Bee Ambrosia

4 TO 6 SERVINGS

4 medium oranges, chilled
1 medium banana
¹/₂ cup orange juice
¹/₄ cup honey
2 tablespoons lemon juice
¹/₄ cup flaked coconut

Pare oranges and cut into thin slices. Peel banana and cut into slices. Mix fruits carefully. Blend orange juice, honey and lemon juice; pour on fruit. Sprinkle with coconut.

Following pages: Sausage-Cheese Biscuit Sandwiches

Fruit and Cereal Coffee Cake

1 COFFEE CAKE

1 cup whole wheat flake cereal
1 cup orange juice
1/4 cup salad oil
1 egg
2 small bananas, thinly sliced
1 1/2 cups all-purpose flour
3/4 cup sugar
1/2 cup raisins, if desired
1 teaspoon baking soda
1 teaspoon cinnamon
1/2 teaspoon salt
Streusel Topping (below)

Heat oven to 350°. Grease square baking pan, 8 × 8 × 2 inches. Mix cereal and orange juice in large mixing bowl; let stand until soft, about 2 minutes. Mix in oil, egg and bananas. Stir in flour, sugar, raisins, baking soda, cinnamon and salt. Spread in pan. Bake until top springs back when touched lightly, about 45 minutes. Sprinkle Streusel Topping evenly over warm coffee cake. Set oven control to broil and/or 550°. Broil 5 inches from heat until bubbly, about 1 minute. (Watch carefully to avoid burning.)

STREUSEL TOPPING

1/2 cup packed brown sugar
1/2 cup chopped nuts
1/4 cup all-purpose or unbleached flour
1/2 teaspoon cinnamon
1/4 cup margarine or butter, softened

Mix all ingredients until crumbly.

Churros

ABOUT 2 DOZEN CHURROS

Vegetable oil
1 cup water
1/2 cup margarine or butter
1 cup all-purpose flour
1/4 teaspoon salt
3 eggs
Powdered sugar or cinnamon-sugar
   mixture

Heat oil (1 1/2 inches) to 375° in 4-quart Dutch oven or deep saucepan. Heat water and margarine to rolling boil in 3-quart saucepan. Remove from heat; quickly stir in flour and salt. Stir vigorously over low heat until mixture forms a ball. Remove from heat; beat in eggs, 1 at a time, until smooth and glossy.

Spoon mixture into pastry bag fitted with star tip #6. Squeeze 5-inch strips of dough into hot oil. Cook, turning frequently, until deep golden brown; drain. Sprinkle generously with powdered sugar. Serve warm.

34   BETTY CROCKER'S RED SPOON COLLECTION

Honey-Cinnamon Syrup

ENOUGH FOR ABOUT 12 PANCAKES

³⁄₄ cup honey
¹⁄₂ cup margarine or butter
¹⁄₂ teaspoon ground cinnamon

Heat all ingredients in 1-quart saucepan, stirring constantly, until hot.

Spicy Cider Syrup

ENOUGH FOR ABOUT 16 PANCAKES

1 cup sugar
3 tablespoons all-purpose flour
¹⁄₄ teaspoon ground cinnamon
¹⁄₄ teaspoon ground nutmeg
2 cups apple cider
2 tablespoons lemon juice
¹⁄₄ cup margarine or butter

Mix sugar, flour, cinnamon and nutmeg in 2-quart saucepan; stir in cider and lemon juice. Cook, stirring constantly, until mixture thickens and boils. Boil and stir 1 minute; remove from heat. Stir in margarine.

Mixed Berry Syrup

ENOUGH FOR ABOUT 16 PANCAKES

1 cup fruit preserves, any flavor
¹⁄₂ cup fresh or frozen (thawed)
  blueberries
2 tablespoons margarine or butter
2 tablespoons water

Heat all ingredients in 1-quart saucepan until margarine is melted and syrup is warm, stirring occasionally.

Very Berry Syrup

ABOUT ¹⁄₂ CUP SYRUP

1 cup maple-flavored syrup
2 tablespoons margarine or butter
2 cups sliced strawberries
1 cup fresh or frozen (thawed and
  drained) blueberries

Heat syrup and margarine in 2-quart saucepan over low heat until margarine is melted. Stir in strawberries and blueberries; heat until hot.

Lemonade

3 cups water
1 cup lemon juice (about 4 lemons)
1/2 cup sugar

Mix all ingredients. Serve over ice.

LIMEADE: Substitute lime juice (about 10 limes) for the lemons and increase sugar to 3/4 cup.

MINTED LEMONADE: Bruise mint leaves in glasses before pouring Lemonade. Garnish with mint leaves.

PINK LEMONADE: Add 2 or 3 drops red food color and, if desired, 2 tablespoons grenadine syrup.

Breakfast Punch

6 SERVINGS

1 1/2 cups orange juice, chilled
1 cup lemon juice, chilled
3 cups apple cider, chilled
1/4 cup sugar

Stir juices and sugar until sugar is dissolved. Pour over ice cubes. Garnish with mint leaves.

BREAKFAST FOR A CROWD

Eggs Benedict

Hollandaise Sauce (below)
6 English muffins
Margarine or butter, softened
12 thin slices fully cooked Canadian-style
bacon or smoked ham
2 teaspoons margarine or butter
12 poached eggs

Prepare Hollandaise Sauce (below); hold sauce over warm water. Split English muffins; toast and spread margarine on each half. Fry bacon in 2 teaspoons margarine until light brown. Prepare poached eggs (page 105). Place 1 bacon slice on cut side of each muffin; top with a poached egg. Spoon warm sauce over eggs.

HOLLANDAISE SAUCE

6 egg yolks
2 tablespoons lemon juice
1 cup firm butter*

Stir egg yolks and lemon juice vigorously in 1½-quart saucepan. Add ¼ cup of the butter. Heat over *very low heat*, stirring constantly with wire whisk, until butter is melted. Add remaining butter. Continue stirring vigorously until butter is melted and sauce is thickened. (Be sure butter melts slowly as this gives eggs time to cook and thicken sauce without curdling.) Cover and refrigerate any remaining sauce.

*Do not use margarine, butter blends or spreads in this recipe.

Following pages: Eggs Benedict, left , and Swiss Fried Potatoes, right (page 50)

Creamed Eggs and Corn Bread

1 large onion, chopped (about ¾ cup)
⅓ cup margarine or butter
⅓ cup all-purpose flour
2 teaspoons dry mustard
1 teaspoon salt
¼ teaspoon pepper
3½ cups milk
2 cups shredded Cheddar cheese
   (8 ounces)
1 package (10 ounces) frozen green peas
12 hard-cooked eggs, sliced
1 can (2¼ ounces) sliced ripe olives
   (about ½ cup)
Corn Bread (below)

Cook and stir onion in margarine in 3-quart saucepan over medium heat until onion is tender, about 5 minutes. Stir in flour, mustard, salt and pepper. Cook over low heat, stirring constantly, until bubbly; remove from heat. Stir in milk. Heat to boiling, stirring constantly. Boil and stir 1 minute. Add cheese; cook and stir until cheese is melted. Rinse peas under running cold water to separate; drain. Stir peas, eggs and olives into cheese sauce. Cover and refrigerate no longer than 24 hours.

Prepare Corn Bread. Cover cheese sauce–egg mixture and heat over medium-low heat, stirring occasionally, until hot, about 25 minutes. Cut warm bread into 12 pieces; serve with cheese sauce–egg mixture.

CORN BREAD

1½ cups cornmeal
½ cup all-purpose flour
2 teaspoons baking powder
1 teaspoon sugar
1 teaspoon salt
½ teaspoon baking soda
¼ cup shortening
1½ cups buttermilk
2 eggs

Heat oven to 450°. Mix all ingredients; beat vigorously 30 seconds. Pour into greased square pan, 9 × 9 × 2 inches. Bake until top springs back when touched lightly in center, about 20 minutes.

Oven Scrambled Eggs

1/4 cup margarine or butter, melted
18 eggs
1 cup milk
1 1/2 teaspoons salt
1/4 to 1/2 teaspoon pepper

Pour margarine into rectangular pan, 13 × 9 × 2 inches; tilt pan to coat bottom. Beat remaining ingredients with rotary beater. Pour into pan. Cover and refrigerate no longer than 24 hours.

Bake uncovered in 350° oven, stirring frequently, until eggs are thickened throughout but still moist, about 30 minutes.

Eggs and Broccoli

2 packages (10 ounces each) frozen chopped broccoli
3/4 teaspoon salt
24 hard-cooked eggs, cut lengthwise into fourths
2 cans (11 ounces each) condensed Cheddar cheese soup
1 1/2 cups milk
2 jars (2 ounces each) diced pimiento, drained
2 teaspoons parsley flakes
1 teaspoon dry mustard
1/2 teaspoon dried basil leaves
1/4 teaspoon onion powder
6 drops red pepper sauce
1 1/2 cups crushed corn chips or potato chips

Heat oven to 350°. Rinse broccoli in cold water to separate; drain. Spread broccoli in ungreased 13 × 9 × 2-inch baking dish; sprinkle with salt. Arrange eggs, cut sides up, on broccoli. Mix soup, milk, pimiento, parsley, mustard, basil, onion powder and pepper sauce; heat to boiling. Pour over eggs. Sprinkle with chips. Cook uncovered in oven until hot, 20 to 25 minutes.

Festival Eggs

¹/₃ cup margarine or butter
¹/₃ cup vegetable oil
12 corn or flour tortillas, cut into thin
*   strips*
2 medium onions, chopped (about 1 cup)
12 eggs, beaten
4 tomatoes, chopped
2 jalapeño peppers, seeded and chopped
4 tablespoons snipped cilantro
1 teaspoon salt
¹/₂ teaspoon pepper
1 cup shredded cheese (about 4 ounces)

Heat margarine and oil in 12-inch skillet over medium heat until hot. Add tortilla strips and onions; cook, turning occasionally, until tortillas are brown. Mix remaining ingredients except cheese; pour into skillet.

As mixture begins to set at bottom and side, gently lift cooked portion with spatula so that thin uncooked portion can flow to bottom. Turn egg mixture; cook just until eggs are set but not dry. Sprinkle with cheese.

Smoky Beef and Cheese Quiche

1¹/₂ cups hot cooked rice
1 tablespoon snipped fresh chives
1 egg white
1 package (2.5 ounces) smoked sliced
*   beef*
3 eggs
1 egg yolk
1 can (13 ounces) evaporated skim milk
¹/₄ teaspoon salt
¹/₂ cup shredded mozzarella or
*   Monterey Jack cheese (2 ounces)*
¹/₄ cup finely chopped onion (about
*   1 small)*
8 tomato slices

Heat oven to 350°. Beat rice, chives and egg white with fork. Turn mixture into pie plate, 10 × 1¹/₂ inches, sprayed with nonstick cooking spray. Spread evenly with rubber spatula on bottom and halfway up side of pie plate (do not leave any holes). Bake 5 minutes.

Cut meat into small pieces and sprinkle in rice crust. Beat eggs, egg yolk, skim milk and salt; stir in cheese and onion. Carefully pour into rice crust. Bake until knife inserted in center comes out clean, 25 to 30 minutes. Immediately run knife around edge to loosen crust. Let stand 10 minutes before serving. Garnish with tomato slices.

Chicken-Gruyère Quiche

Pastry for 9-inch one-crust pie
6 slices bacon, cut into 1/2-inch pieces
1 small onion, chopped (about 1/4 cup)
1 cup cut-up cooked chicken
1 cup shredded Gruyère or Swiss cheese
  (4 ounces)
2 tablespoons snipped parsley
5 eggs
1 1/4 cups half-and-half
1/2 cup dry white wine
1/4 teaspoon pepper
1/8 teaspoon salt

Place oven rack in lowest position. Heat oven to 425°. Fold pastry into fourths; unfold and ease into ungreased quiche dish, 9 × 1 1/2 inches, or pie plate, 9 × 1 1/4 inches, pressing firmly against bottom and sides. Trim overhanging edge of pastry 1 inch from rim of dish. Fold and roll pastry under to make it even with dish; flute edge.

Cook and stir bacon over medium heat until almost crisp; stir in onion. Cook until onion is tender; drain.

Sprinkle chicken, cheese and parsley in pastry. Beat remaining ingredients until blended; stir in bacon mixture. Place quiche dish on oven rack; pour egg-bacon mixture over cheese. Bake 15 minutes.

Reduce oven temperature to 300°. Bake until knife inserted in center comes out clean, about 30 minutes longer. Let stand 10 minutes before cutting.

Seafood Crepes

Crepes (below)
1/4 cup chopped fresh mushrooms (about 3 medium)
2 tablespoons chopped green onion
2 tablespoons margarine or butter
2/3 cup small cooked shrimp
1 package (6 ounces) frozen crabmeat, thawed and drained
1/2 cup half-and-half
2 packages (3 ounces each) cream cheese, cubed
1 cup shredded Swiss cheese (4 ounces)
2 tablespoons chopped green onion

CREPES

2/3 cup all-purpose flour
1 cup milk
1 tablespoon vegetable oil
1 teaspoon sugar
1/4 teaspoon baking powder
1/4 teaspoon salt
1 egg

Prepare Crepes. Cook and stir mushrooms and 2 tablespoons onion in margarine until onion is tender. Stir in seafood, half-and-half and cream cheese. Cook over medium heat, stirring constantly, until cheese is melted.

Spoon about 1/4 cup filling down center of each crepe; roll up. Place in dish; sprinkle with Swiss cheese. Cover with heavy-duty aluminum foil.

Heat oven to 350°. Bake until hot and cheese is melted, about 20 minutes. Sprinkle crepes with 2 tablespoons onion.

Beat all ingredients with hand beater until smooth. For each crepe, lightly butter 7-inch or 8-inch skillet; heat over medium heat until bubbly.

Pour scant 1/4 cup batter into skillet; rotate skillet until batter covers bottom. Cook until light brown; turn and cook other side until light brown.

Stack crepes, placing waxed paper between each. Keep crepes covered to prevent them from drying out.

Texas Breakfast Tacos

Southwest Guacamole (page 57)
Fresh Tomato Salsa (page 57)
1 pound bulk chorizo sausage
1 large onion, finely chopped (about
*   1 cup)*
1 medium green bell pepper, cut into
*   strips*
1 tablespoon margarine or butter
12 eggs, beaten
10 flour tortillas (7 to 8 inches in
*   diameter), warmed*
1½ cups shredded Co-Jack cheese
*   (6 ounces)*
2 tablespoons margarine or butter, melted

Prepare Southwest Guacamole and Fresh Tomato Salsa; reserve. Cook and stir sausage, onion and bell pepper in 10-inch skillet over medium heat, stirring frequently, until sausage is done, about 10 minutes; drain and reserve.

Heat 1 tablespoon margarine in skillet over medium heat until hot and bubbly. Pour eggs into skillet. As eggs begin to set at bottom and side, gently lift cooked portions with spatula so that thin, uncooked portion can flow to bottom. Avoid constant stirring. Cook until eggs are thickened throughout but still moist, about 5 minutes.

Heat oven to 450°. Spoon about ¼ cup sausage mixture onto each tortilla; top each with about ¼ cup eggs and 2 tablespoons cheese. Fold tortillas into halves. Arrange 5 assembled tacos in ungreased jelly roll pan, 15½ × 10½ × 1 inch; brush with melted margarine. Bake until light golden brown, 10 to 12 minutes. Repeat with remaining tacos. Serve with guacamole and salsa.

Following pages: Southwest Guacamole, left (page 57), Fresh Tomato Salsa, middle (page 57) and Texas Breakfast Tacos, right

Cooked Smoked Ham Slices

*2 fully cooked smoked ham slices, 1 inch
thick (each about 2 pounds)*

Slash diagonally outer edge of fat of each ham slice at 1-inch intervals to prevent curling.

TO BAKE: Place ham slices in ungreased baking dish. Bake uncovered in 325° oven 30 minutes.

TO BROIL: Set oven control to broil and/or 550°. Broil ham slices with top about 3 inches from heat until light brown, about 10 minutes. Turn; broil until light brown, about 6 minutes longer. Brush ham with 3 tablespoons jelly, slightly beaten, during last 2 minutes of broiling, if desired.

Prosciutto Salad with Grapefruit-Honey Dressing

6 SERVINGS

*3 grapefruit
Grapefruit-Honey Dressing (below)
³/₄ pound prosciutto or thinly sliced fully
    cooked smoked ham
Salad greens
4 unpared eating apples, sliced*

Pare and section grapefruit, allowing juice to drain into bowl. Reserve ⅓ cup of the juice for Grapefruit-Honey Dressing; prepare dressing. Roll up prosciutto.

Arrange salad greens on platter or 4 salad plates. Arrange grapefruit, apples and prosciutto on greens. Serve with dressing.

GRAPEFRUIT-HONEY DRESSING

*¹/₃ cup reserved grapefruit juice
4 tablespoons honey
4 tablespoons vegetable oil or sour cream
¹/₄ teaspoon celery seed*

Shake all ingredients in tightly covered container. Shake before using.

Sausage Ring

12 SERVINGS

3 pounds bulk pork sausage
1 1/2 cups soft bread crumbs
1/3 cup snipped parsley
3/4 teaspoon ground sage
3 eggs, slightly beaten
1 medium onion, chopped (about 1/2 cup)

Mix all ingredients. Press lightly in ungreased 9-cup ring mold. Cover and refrigerate no longer than 24 hours.

Unmold sausage mixture on rack in shallow baking pan; cover loosely with aluminum foil. Bake in 350° oven 30 minutes; remove foil. Bake until done, about 30 minutes longer.

Minted Cottage Cheese Salad with Fruit

12 SERVINGS

2 containers (24 ounces each) small
    curd creamed cottage cheese
3 tablespoons snipped fresh mint leaves
Lettuce leaves
3 cups blueberries, raspberries or
    blackberries
1 1/2 pints medium strawberries (about
    3 cups) or 3 large peaches or
    nectarines, sliced
6 medium bananas, sliced
Coarsely chopped salted or toasted nuts
Ginger-Honey Dressing (below)

Mix cottage cheese and mint. Divide lettuce leaves among 4 salad plates. Spoon cheese mixture onto each. Arrange fruit on top; sprinkle with nuts. Serve with Ginger-Honey Dressing.

GINGER-HONEY DRESSING

3/4 cup vegetable oil
3/4 cup lime juice
3/4 cup honey
6 tablespoons mayonnaise or salad
    dressing
1/2 teaspoon salt
3/4 teaspoon ground ginger

Shake all ingredients in tightly covered container.

Swiss Fried Potatoes

6 SERVINGS

4 medium potatoes (about 1½ pounds)
¼ cup margarine or butter
1 small onion, chopped
½ cup diced Gruyère or Swiss cheese
½ teaspoon salt
¼ teaspoon pepper
2 tablespoons water

Heat 1 inch salted water (½ teaspoon salt to 1 cup water) to boiling. Add potatoes. Heat to boiling; reduce heat. Cover and cook until tender, 30 to 35 minutes. Peel and shred potatoes or cut into ¼-inch strips.

Heat margarine in 10-inch skillet until melted. Add potatoes, onion and cheese. Sprinkle with salt and pepper. Cook uncovered over medium heat, turning frequently, until potatoes start to brown, about 10 minutes. (Add 1 to 2 tablespoons margarine to prevent sticking if necessary.)

Press potatoes with spatula to form flat cake; sprinkle with water. Cover and cook over low heat, without stirring, until bottom is golden brown and crusty, about 10 minutes. Place inverted platter over skillet; invert potatoes onto platter.

Avocado-Citrus Salad

6 SERVINGS

1 ripe avocado
Lemon juice
Salt
2 oranges or grapefruit
Watercress or parsley sprigs
Limeade or Lemonade Dressing (below)

Cut avocado in half crosswise; remove pit. Peel each half; cut into ¼-inch slices. Sprinkle slices with lemon juice and salt.

Pare and section oranges or grapefruit. Arrange avocado slices and fruit sections; garnish with watercress. Serve with dressing.

LIMEADE OR LEMONADE DRESSING

⅓ cup frozen limeade or lemonade
  concentrate (thawed)
⅓ cup honey
⅓ cup salad oil
1 teaspoon celery or poppy seed

Blend all ingredients with rotary beater.

Fruit in Honeydew Shells

*1 large honeydew melon (about 7 inches
  in diameter)*
*1/2 small pineapple, cut into bite-size
  pieces*
1/2 pound red seedless grapes
*1 pound green seedless grapes, separated
  into small clusters*
*1 small cantaloupe, cut into bite-size
  pieces*

Cut top third from honeydew melon, using a deep zigzag cut. Cover and refrigerate top portion to use as desired. Remove seeds and scoop balls from larger section of melon; reserve melon balls. Scoop remaining pulp from melon with large spoon to form shell; drain shell. Cut thin slice from bottom of shell to keep it from tipping. Cover and refrigerate no longer than 24 hours. Mix melon balls with remaining ingredients. Cover and refrigerate no longer than 24 hours.

Just before serving, spoon fruit mixture into shell. Garnish with mint leaves, if desired, and serve with wooden picks.

Popovers

1 egg
2 egg whites
1 cup all-purpose flour
1 cup milk
1/4 teaspoon salt

Heat oven to 450°. Spray six 6-ounce custard cups with nonstick cooking spray. Place all ingredients in blender container. Cover and blend on medium speed just until smooth, about 15 seconds, stopping blender to scrape sides if necessary.

Fill custard cups about half full. Bake 20 minutes. Decrease oven temperature to 350°. Bake until deep golden brown, 15 to 20 minutes longer. Immediately remove from cups; serve hot.

Swirl Coffee Cake

1½ cups sugar
½ cup margarine or butter, softened
½ cup shortening
1½ teaspoons baking powder
1 teaspoon vanilla
1 teaspoon almond extract
4 eggs
3 cups all-purpose flour
1 can (21 ounces) cherry, apricot or
* blueberry pie filling*
Glaze (below)

Heat oven to 350°. Generously grease jelly roll pan, 15½ × 10½ × 1 inch, or 2 square pans, 9 × 9 × 2 inches. Blend sugar, margarine, shortening, baking powder, vanilla, almond extract and eggs in large bowl on low speed, scraping bowl constantly. Beat on high speed, scraping bowl occasionally, 3 minutes. Stir in flour. Spread ⅔ of the batter in jelly roll pan or ⅓ in each square pan. Spread pie filling over batter. Drop remaining batter by tablespoonfuls onto pie filling.

Bake until light golden brown, about 45 minutes. Cover and store at room temperature.

Heat covered in 325° oven until warm, about 10 minutes. Prepare Glaze; drizzle over warm coffee cake. Cut cake in jelly roll pan into 3-inch squares; cut cake in square pans into 2¾-inch squares.

GLAZE

1 cup powdered sugar
1 to 2 tablespoons milk

Mix powdered sugar and milk until mixture is smooth and desired consistency.

Scones

¹/₃ cup margarine, butter or shortening
1³/₄ cups all-purpose flour
3 tablespoons sugar
2¹/₂ teaspoons baking powder
¹/₂ teaspoon salt
1 egg, beaten
¹/₂ cup currants or raisins
4 to 6 tablespoons half-and-half
1 egg, beaten
Margarine or butter, softened
Strawberry preserves

Heat oven to 400°. Cut ¹/₃ cup margarine into flour, sugar, baking powder and salt until mixture resembles fine crumbs. Stir in 1 egg, the currants and just enough half-and-half so dough leaves side of bowl. Turn dough onto lightly floured surface. Knead lightly 10 times. Roll ¹/₂ inch thick.

Cut dough into 2-inch circles with floured cutter. Place on ungreased cookie sheet. Brush with 1 egg. Bake until golden, 10 to 12 minutes. Split warm scones; spread with margarine. Serve with strawberry preserves.

Cranberry Muffins

1 cup plain yogurt
3 tablespoons margarine, melted
1 teaspoon grated lemon peel
2 teaspoons lemon juice
1 egg
1¹/₂ cups all-purpose flour
3 tablespoons sugar
1 teaspoon baking powder
1 teaspoon baking soda
²/₃ cup coarsely chopped fresh or frozen
  cranberries
1 tablespoon sugar
Ground nutmeg, if desired

Heat oven to 400°. Spray 12 medium muffin cups, 2¹/₂ × 1¹/₄ inches, with nonstick cooking spray or line with paper baking cups. Beat yogurt, margarine, lemon peel, lemon juice and egg until smooth. Stir in flour, 3 tablespoons sugar, the baking powder and baking soda all at once, just until flour is moistened (batter will be lumpy). Fold in cranberries. Fill cups about ³/₄ full; sprinkle with 1 tablespoon sugar and the nutmeg. Bake until golden brown, 18 to 20 minutes. Immediately remove from pan.

TO MICROWAVE: Prepare microwavable muffin ring and batter as directed. Microwave 6 muffins at a time uncovered on high 1 minute; rotate ring ¹/₂ turn. Microwave until tops are almost dry, 1 to 2 minutes longer. Let stand 1 minute; remove to rack.

Following pages: Scones, left, Swirl Coffee Cake, middle and Cranberry Muffins, upper middle

Blue Cornmeal Muffins

2 eggs
1½ cups milk
3 tablespoons vegetable oil
2 tablespoons finely chopped canned green
    chilies, drained
1¼ cups blue cornmeal
¾ cup all-purpose flour
2 teaspoons baking powder
½ teaspoon salt

Heat oven to 400°. Generously grease about 18 medium muffin cups, 2½ × 1¼ inches. Beat eggs in large bowl; stir in milk, oil and chilies. Stir in remaining ingredients, all at once, just until cornmeal is moistened (batter will be lumpy). Fill muffin cups about ¾ full. Cover and refrigerate remaining batter.

Bake until light golden brown, about 20 minutes. Loosen edges with knife; immediately remove from pan.

Oat-Peach Muffins

1 cup quick-cooking oats
1 cup buttermilk
¼ cup vegetable oil
2 tablespoons light molasses
1 teaspoon vanilla
1 egg
1¼ cups all-purpose flour
¾ cup ¼-inch pieces fresh peaches*
¾ cup coarsely chopped walnuts
¼ cup packed brown sugar
1½ teaspoons ground cinnamon
1 teaspoon baking soda
1 teaspoon baking powder
½ teaspoon salt

Heat oven to 400°. Grease bottoms only of 12 medium muffin cups, 2½ × 1¼ inches. Mix oats and buttermilk in large bowl; beat in oil, molasses, vanilla and egg with fork. Stir in remaining ingredients just until flour is moistened.

Divide batter among muffin cups (cups will be full). Bake until wooden pick inserted in center comes out clean, 15 to 20 minutes. Immediately remove from cups.

*Canned peaches, well drained, or frozen peaches, thawed and well drained, can be used.

OAT-DATE MUFFINS: Substitute chopped dates for the peaches.

OAT-RAISIN MUFFINS: Substitute raisins for the peaches.

Refried Black Beans

1 medium onion, chopped (about ½ cup)
4 jalapeño chilies, seeded and finely
  chopped
4 cloves garlic, finely chopped
4 tablespoons vegetable oil
4 cans (15 ounces each) black beans,
  undrained
2 canned chipotle chilies in adobo sauce,
  chopped
2 teaspoons ground red chilies
¾ teaspoon salt

Cook and stir onion, jalapeño chilies and garlic in oil in 10-inch skillet over medium heat until onion is tender. Stir in remaining ingredients; mash beans.

Cook uncovered, stirring occasionally, until thick, about 15 minutes.

Southwest Guacamole

5 ripe avocados, peeled and pitted
4 cloves garlic, finely chopped
1 medium tomato, chopped (about 1 cup)
¼ cup lime juice
½ teaspoon salt

Mash avocados in a medium bowl until slightly lumpy. Stir in remaining ingredients. Cover and refrigerate 1 hour.

Fresh Tomato Salsa

3 medium tomatoes, seeded and chopped
  (about 3 cups)
½ cup sliced green onions (with tops)
½ cup chopped green bell pepper
2 to 3 tablespoons lime juice
2 tablespoons snipped fresh cilantro
1 tablespoon finely chopped jalapeño
  chili
1 teaspoon finely chopped garlic (about
  3 cloves)
½ teaspoon salt

Mix all ingredients.

Citus Spread

ABOUT 1 CUP

1 cup margarine or butter, softened
2 tablespoons orange peel

Beat margarine and orange peel in small bowl on high speed until blended.

Lemon-Cheese Spread

1 CUP SPREAD

1 package (8 ounces) cream cheese,
   softened
1 tablespoon powdered sugar
1 teaspoon grated lemon peel
1 tablespoon lemon juice

Beat all ingredients on medium speed until fluffy.

Fruited Cream Cheese Spread

1 1/4 CUPS SPREAD

1 package (8 ounces) cream cheese,
   softened
1/4 cup peach preserves

Beat cream cheese and preserves on medium speed until fluffy.

Vegetable Spread

ABOUT 1/2 CUP

1 package (3 ounces) cream cheese,
   softened
1 tablespoon finely chopped broccoli
1 tablespoon finely chopped carrot
1/2 teaspoon minced onion

Mix all ingredients until blended.

Mimosa

1/3 cup sugar
2 2/3 cups fresh orange juice, chilled
2 bottles (750 ml each) champagne,
   chilled
8 orange slices
8 mint sprigs

Place sugar and orange juice in blender container. Cover and blend on medium speed until foamy, about 15 seconds. Pour 1/3 cup into each of 8 tall glasses; add about 1 cup champagne to each. Garnish with orange slice and mint sprig.

Hot Orange Cider

1 can (12 ounces) frozen orange juice
   concentrate
1 1/2 quarts apple cider
1/2 cup rum, if desired
1 orange, cut into 12 slices

Prepare orange juice as directed on can. Heat orange juice and apple cider over low heat just to boiling. Pour about 1 cup orange juice mixture into each of 12 mugs. Stir 2 teaspoons rum in each; top with orange slice. Garnish with stick cinnamon, if desired.

Fresh Fruit Frappé

1 cup cut-up watermelon
1 cup cut-up cantaloupe or honeydew
   melon
1 cup cut-up pineapple
1 cup cut-up mango
1 cup strawberry halves
1/4 cup sugar
1 cup orange juice
Crushed ice

Mix all ingredients except ice. Fill blender container half full of mixture; add crushed ice to fill to top. Cover and blend on high speed until uniform consistency.

Repeat with remaining mixture. Serve immediately; garnish with fruit, if desired.

Salt-rimmed Tomato Juice

6 SERVINGS

2 cans (11½ ounces each) tomato juice
2 tablespoons lemon juice
½ teaspoon Worcestershire sauce
1 drop red pepper sauce
Lemon wedges
Salt

Mix tomato juice, lemon juice, the Worcestershire sauce and pepper sauce. Refrigerate. Before serving, rub rim of each glass with lemon wedge; dip rims in salt. Fill glasses with chilled juice.

Fiesta Hot Chocolate

10 SERVINGS

1 cup cocoa
2 tablespoons all-purpose flour
⅔ cup grated piloncillo or ¼ cup packed
  dark brown sugar
8 cups milk
6 whole cloves
2 sticks cinnamon, broken into halves
4 tablespoons powdered sugar
1 tablespoon vanilla
Whipped cream
10 sticks cinnamon

Mix cocoa and flour in 2-quart saucepan. Stir in piloncillo, milk, cloves and 2 sticks cinnamon. Heat just to boiling over medium heat, stirring constantly; reduce heat. Simmer uncovered 5 minutes (do not boil). Remove from heat; remove cloves and cinnamon. Stir in powdered sugar and vanilla.

Beat with molinillo, wire whisk or hand beater until foamy. Pour into 10 cups or mugs. Serve with whipped cream and cinnamon sticks.

Café au Lait

12 SERVINGS

4½ cups strong coffee
4½ cups hot milk

Pour equal amounts of hot coffee and hot milk simultaneously from separate pots into each cup.

International Coffee

1 cup instant cocoa mix
¾ cup instant coffee
12 cups boiling water
Sweetened whipped cream

Mix cocoa and coffee in a large serving pot. Pour in boiling water; stir. Serve steaming hot and top with whipped cream.

Arctic Coffee

1 cup sifted powdered sugar
5 teaspoons vanilla
8 cups double strength coffee (chilled)
¼ teaspoon cinnamon
Dash of nutmeg
1 cup whipping cream
Coffee ice cubes

Add powdered sugar and vanilla to chilled coffee. Mix until sugar is dissolved. Add spices to whipping cream; chill. Just before serving whip until stiff. Pour coffee over coffee ice cubes and top with whipped cream.

Note: To make coffee ice cubes, freeze 4 cups regular strength coffee in 2 trays.

· 4 ·

LAZY DAY BREAKFASTS

Oven Omelet

¼ cup margarine or butter
18 eggs
1 cup dairy sour cream
1 cup milk
2 teaspoons salt
¼ cup chopped green onions (with tops)

Heat oven to 325°. Heat margarine in rectangular baking dish, 13 × 9 × 2 inches, in oven until melted. Tilt dish to coat bottom. Beat eggs, sour cream, milk and salt until blended. Stir in onions. Pour into dish.

Bake until eggs are set but moist, about 35 minutes. Cut into serving pieces.

Potatoes and Eggs

12 ounces bulk pork sausage
1 small onion, chopped
3 cups frozen shredded hash brown
  potatoes
1 teaspoon herb-seasoned salt
1½ cups shredded Swiss cheese (6 ounces)
6 eggs

Heat oven to 350°. Cook and stir sausage and onion in 10-inch skillet over medium heat until sausage is brown; drain. Stir in frozen potatoes and herb-seasoned salt. Cook, stirring constantly, just until potatoes are thawed, about 2 minutes. Remove from heat; stir in cheese. Spread in ungreased rectangular baking dish, 11 × 7 × 1½ inches.

Make 6 indentations in potato mixture with back of spoon; break 1 egg into each indentation. Bake uncovered until eggs are desired doneness, 20 to 25 minutes.

Ranch-style Eggs

Mexican Sauce (below)
Vegetable oil
8 tortillas (4 inches in diameter)
Vegetable oil
8 eggs
Salt and pepper
1 cup shredded Monterey Jack cheese
   (4 ounces)

Prepare Mexican Sauce. Heat oil (⅛ inch) in 6- or 8-inch skillet until hot. Cook tortillas until crisp and light brown, about 1 minute on each side. Drain on paper towels; keep warm.

Heat oil (⅛ inch) in 12-inch skillet until hot. Break each egg into measuring cup or saucer; carefully slip 4 eggs, 1 at a time, into skillet. Immediately reduce heat. Cook slowly, spooning oil onto eggs until whites are set and a film forms over the yolks. Or turn eggs over gently when whites are set and cook to desired doneness. Sprinkle with salt and pepper. Repeat with remaining eggs.

Spoon 1 tablespoon sauce over each tortilla; place 1 egg on each. Spoon sauce over white of egg; sprinkle yolk with cheese.

MEXICAN SAUCE

1 medium onion, chopped
½ green pepper, chopped
1 clove garlic, finely chopped
1 tablespoon vegetable oil
2 cups chopped ripe tomatoes*
¼ to ½ cup chopped green chilies
5 drops red pepper sauce
½ teaspoon sugar
⅛ teaspoon salt

Cook and stir onion, green pepper and garlic in oil in 2-quart saucepan until green pepper is tender, about 5 minutes. Stir in remaining ingredients. Heat to boiling; reduce heat. Simmer uncovered until slightly thickened, about 15 minutes.

*1 can (16 ounces) tomatoes (with liquid) can be substituted for the ripe tomatoes. Break up tomatoes.

Following pages: Quick Chili-Cheese Puff, left (page 67), and Oven Omelet, right

Eggs and Corn Scramble

2 tablespoons margarine or butter
8 eggs, slightly beaten
1 can (11 ounces) whole kernel corn with
    peppers
1 cup shredded Cheddar cheese (about
    4 ounces)
1/2 cup milk
1/2 teaspoon dried basil leaves
1/2 teaspoon salt
1/8 teaspoon pepper

Heat margarine in 10-inch skillet over medium heat until melted. Mix remaining ingredients; pour into skillet. As mixture begins to set at bottom and side, gently lift cooked portions with spatula so that thin, uncooked portion can flow to bottom. Avoid constant stirring. Cook until eggs are thickened throughout but still moist, 5 to 8 minutes.

TO MICROWAVE: Place margarine in 2-quart microwavable casserole. Microwave uncovered on high until melted, 30 to 45 seconds. Mix remaining ingredients; pour into casserole. Microwave, uncovered, stirring every 2 minutes, until eggs are set but still moist, 8 to 10 minutes. (Eggs will continue to cook while standing.)

Maple-Bacon Oven Pancake

1 1/2 cups variety baking mix
1 tablespoon sugar
1 1/2 cups shredded Cheddar or process
    American cheese (6 ounces)
3/4 cup milk
1/4 cup maple-flavored syrup
2 eggs
12 slices bacon (about 1/2 pound), crisply
    cooked and crumbled

Heat oven to 425°. Grease and flour rectangular baking dish, 13 × 9 × 2 inches. Beat baking mix, sugar, 1/2 cup of the cheese, the milk, syrup and eggs with hand beater until smooth; pour into dish. Bake uncovered until wooden pick inserted in center comes out clean, 10 to 15 minutes.

Sprinkle pancake with remaining cheese and the bacon. Bake uncovered until cheese is melted, 3 to 5 minutes longer. Serve with maple-flavored syrup, if desired.

Easy Popover Pancake

3 tablespoons margarine or butter
2 eggs
1/2 cup milk
1/2 cup all-purpose flour
1/4 teaspoon ground cinnamon, if desired

Heat oven to 400°. Heat margarine in 1-quart shallow round casserole or 8-inch ovenproof skillet in oven until melted. Place remaining ingredients in blender container in order listed. Cover and blend on high speed 15 seconds. Scrape sides; stir to moisten any remaining flour. Or beat ingredients with hand beater until smooth. Pour into casserole.

Bake until center is puffed and edge is golden brown, 20 to 25 minutes. Serve with fresh fruit and sweetened whipped cream or yogurt, if desired.

Quick Chili-Cheese Puff

1 cup shredded sharp Cheddar cheese
   (4 ounces)
2 cans (4 ounces each) whole green
   chilies, drained
1/4 cup all-purpose flour
1/2 cup milk
1/4 teaspoon pepper
2 eggs

Heat oven to 350°. Layer half of the cheese, the chilies and remaining cheese in 1-quart casserole or four 10-ounce custard cups sprayed with nonstick cooking spray. Beat remaining ingredients with rotary beater until smooth; pour over top. Bake until puffy and golden brown, casserole about 40 minutes, custard cups about 20 minutes.

Sausage with Peaches

1 pound fully cooked kielbasa or Polish
   sausage, cut into 1-inch slices
1 can (16 ounces) sliced peaches, drained

Cook sausage in 12-inch skillet over medium-high heat, turning occasionally, until brown, about 10 minutes. Add peaches; reduce heat. Cover and heat over low heat until peaches are hot, about 5 minutes.

Following pages: Ranch-style Eggs, left (page 63), and Easy Popover Pancake, right

Fruit-Cheese Kabobs with Ginger Dip

Ginger Dip (below)
24 seedless green grapes
24 pineapple chunks, each about ¾ inch
wide (¼ pineapple)
24 mandarin orange segments or 1 can
(11 ounces) mandarin orange segments,
drained
12 strawberries, each cut into halves
24 cheese cubes, each about ¾ inch thick
(about 8 ounces caraway, Colby,
Cheddar, Monterey Jack or cream
cheese)

Prepare Ginger Dip. Alternate 5 pieces of any combination of fruit and cheese on plastic or wooden picks. Serve with Ginger Dip.

GINGER DIP

ABOUT 3 CUPS DIP

1 package (8 ounces) cream cheese,
softened
1 cup plain yogurt
¼ cup honey
2 teaspoons crushed gingerroot
1 can (8 ounces) crushed pineapple in
juice, drained

Beat cream cheese, yogurt, honey and gingerroot until creamy. Fold in pineapple. Cover; refrigerate 1 hour.

Oven Bacon

12 slices bacon (about 1½ pounds)

Place bacon slices on rack in broiler pan and on wire rack in jelly roll pan, 15½ × 10½ × 1 inch (do not overlap slices). Bake in 400° oven, without turning, until light brown, 15 to 20 minutes. Cool slightly; remove from racks. Cover and refrigerate no longer than 24 hours.

Heat oven to 450°. Place bacon slices in jelly roll pan, 15½ × 10½ × 1 inch. Bake until hot and crisp, about 5 minutes.

Potatoes O'Brien

1/3 cup chopped green bell pepper
2 tablespoons chopped pimiento
1 medium onion, chopped
1/4 cup margarine or butter
1 package (16 ounces) frozen French fried
    potatoes, diced
1/2 teaspoon salt
1/8 teaspoon pepper

Cook and stir bell pepper, pimiento and onion in margarine in 10-inch skillet until onion is tender. Stir in potatoes, salt and pepper. Cook, stirring occasionally, until potatoes are brown and heated.

Broiled Honey Grapefruit

3 grapefruit, halved
1/4 cup plus 2 tablespoons honey
15 drops aromatic bitters

Remove seeds from grapefruit halves. Cut around edges and sections to loosen; remove centers. Mix honey and bitters; spoon about 1 tablespoon honey mixture on each grapefruit half.

Set oven control at broil and/or 550°. Broil grapefruit 5 inches from heat about 5 minutes.

Baked Bananas

4 large, firm bananas, cut lengthwise
    into halves
Lemon juice
4 teaspoons grated lemon peel
4 tablespoons brown sugar
2 tablespoons margarine or butter, melted

Heat oven to 375°. Place banana halves cut side down in buttered baking dish. Brush with lemon juice. Sprinkle each half with 1/2 teaspoon grated lemon peel and 1/2 tablespoon brown sugar. Drizzle each banana with 1/2 tablespoon margarine, melted. Bake 20 minutes. Serve warm.

Pretty Fruit Salad

2 cups seedless grapes
2 cans (11 ounces each) mandarin orange
    segments, chilled and drained
2 cans (8 ounces each) pineapple chunks
    in syrup, chilled and drained
2 red apples, sliced
Salad greens

Mix grapes, orange segments, pineapple and apple. Spoon onto salad greens.

Spicy Peach Salad

2 cans (16 ounces each) peach halves,
    drained (reserve ¼ cup syrup)
1 cup water
2 tablespoons lemon juice
1 stick cinnamon, broken into 1-inch
    pieces
8 whole cloves
¼ teaspoon ground ginger
2 cans (20 ounces each) sliced pineapple,
    drained
Salad greens
Strawberry or raspberry preserves or jam

Heat peaches, reserved peach syrup, the water, lemon juice, cinnamon, cloves and ginger in saucepan to boiling, stirring gently. Reduce heat; simmer uncovered 10 minutes. Spoon peaches and spices into pint jar. Pour hot syrup over peaches. Cover and refrigerate at least 4 hours but no longer than 4 days.

Arrange pineapple slices on salad greens. Place 1 peach half cut side up on each pineapple slice and spoon about ½ teaspoon preserves into center.

Stir and Drop Biscuits

1¾ cups all-purpose flour
2 teaspoons baking powder
1 teaspoon salt
¼ teaspoon baking soda
⅓ cup vegetable oil
⅔ cup buttermilk

Heat oven to 475°. Mix flour, baking powder, salt and baking soda. Pour oil and buttermilk into measuring cup (do not stir together); pour all at once into flour mixture. Stir until mixture cleans side of bowl and forms a ball. Drop dough onto ungreased cookie sheet. Bake 10 to 12 minutes.

Buttermilk-Cereal Muffins

1 egg
¾ cup buttermilk
⅓ cup shortening
1 cup slightly crushed toasted whole grain
  wheat flake cereal (about 2 cups
  uncrushed)
1¼ cups all-purpose flour
½ cup sugar
1 teaspoon baking powder
½ teaspoon salt
½ teaspoon baking soda

Heat oven to 375°. Grease bottoms of 12 muffin cups, 2½ × 1¼ inches. Beat egg in medium bowl; mix in buttermilk and shortening. Stir in remaining ingredients just until moistened. Fill muffin cups about ⅔ full. Bake until golden brown, 15 to 20 minutes. Immediately remove from pan.

Jam Crumpets

6 English muffins, split
¼ cup margarine or butter, softened
¼ cup jam or preserves
¼ cup packed brown sugar
¼ cup flaked coconut or sliced almonds

Heat oven to 450°. Spread cut surface of each muffin half with 1 teaspoon each margarine and jam. Sprinkle with brown sugar and coconut. Bake on ungreased cookie sheet 5 minutes or until bubbly and brown.

Following pages: Pretty Fruit Salad, left, and Buttermilk-Cereal Muffins, right

Overnight Cinnamon Rolls

2 packages active dry yeast
½ cup warm water (105° to 115°)
2 cups lukewarm milk (scalded, then
   cooled)
⅓ cup sugar
⅓ cup vegetable oil or shortening
3 teaspoons baking powder
2 teaspoons salt
1 egg
6½ to 7½ cups all-purpose flour
¼ cup margarine or butter, softened
½ cup sugar
1 tablespoon plus 1 teaspoon ground
   cinnamon
Powdered Sugar Frosting (below)

Dissolve yeast in warm water in large bowl. Stir in milk, ⅓ cup sugar, the oil, baking powder, salt, egg and 3 cups of the flour. Beat until smooth. Stir in enough remaining flour to make dough easy to handle.

Turn dough onto well-floured surface; knead until smooth and elastic, 8 to 10 minutes. Place in greased bowl; turn greased side up. Cover; let rise in warm place until double, about 1½ hours. (Dough is ready if indentation remains when touched.)

Punch down dough; divide into halves. Roll 1 half into rectangle, 12 × 10 inches. Spread with half of the margarine. Mix ½ cup sugar and the cinnamon; sprinkle half of the sugar-cinnamon mixture over rectangle. Roll up, beginning at 12-inch side. Pinch edge of dough into roll to seal. Stretch roll to make even.

Cut roll into 12 slices. Place slightly apart in greased baking pan 13 × 9 × 2 inches. Wrap pan tightly with heavy-duty aluminum foil. Repeat with remaining dough. Refrigerate at least 12 hours but no longer than 48 hours. (To bake immediately, do not wrap. Let rise in warm place until double, about 30 minutes. Bake as directed below.)

Heat oven to 350°. Remove foil from pans. Bake until golden, 30 to 35 minutes. Frost with Powdered Sugar Frosting while warm.

POWDERED SUGAR FROSTING

2 cups powdered sugar
2 tablespoons milk
1 teaspoon vanilla

Mix powdered sugar, milk and vanilla until smooth and of spreading consistency.

Cinnamon Spread

¾ *cup granola, slightly crushed*
½ *cup peanut butter*
½ *teaspoon ground cinnamon*

Mix all ingredients; spread on split bagels or English muffins.

BROILED GRANOLA-CINNAMON SPREAD: Set oven control to broil and/or 550°. After spreading granola mixture on toast or bread, broil 3 inches from heat until bubbly and light brown.

Tomato Bouillon

1½ *cups tomato juice*
½ *cup water*
2 *teaspoons instant beef bouillon*

Heat all ingredients to boiling over medium-high heat, stirring occasionally. Serve hot or cold.

· 5 ·

HOLIDAY BREAKFASTS

Sherried Eggs and Asparagus

4 SERVINGS

¼ cup dry sherry or dry white wine
1 tablespoon margarine or butter
6 hard-cooked eggs, peeled and cut
  lengthwise into halves
1 cup half-and-half
¼ teaspoon salt
⅛ teaspoon freshly ground pepper
1 tablespoon all-purpose flour
2 tablespoons dry sherry or dry white
  wine
4 slices whole wheat bread, toasted
1 package (10 ounces) frozen asparagus
  spears or 1 pound fresh asparagus,
  cooked

Heat ¼ cup sherry and the margarine in
10-inch skillet over medium heat until margarine is melted. Place peeled eggs, cut sides
down, in skillet; reduce heat. Simmer uncovered until heated through, about 5 minutes.
Remove eggs; keep warm. Stir half-and-half,
salt and pepper into sherry mixture in skillet.
Shake flour and 2 tablespoons wine in tightly
covered container; stir into half-and-half mixture. Heat to boiling over medium heat, stirring constantly. Boil and stir 1 minute.

Cut each slice bread into 4 triangles. Arrange
3 egg halves, cut side up, and several asparagus spears on each serving plate. Place 4 toast
triangles on each plate. Spoon some sauce over
eggs. Serve with remaining sauce.

Eggs with Wine Sauce

½ cup sliced green onions (with tops)
6 tablespoons margarine or butter
6 tablespoons all-purpose flour
1 teaspoon dry mustard
½ teaspoon dried tarragon leaves
¼ teaspoon white pepper
1½ cups dry white wine
1½ cups chicken broth
12 slices bacon, crisply fried and crumbled
16 eggs
8 croissants, split*

Cook and stir onions in margarine in 1-quart saucepan over medium heat 3 minutes. Blend in flour, mustard, tarragon and pepper. Cook over low heat, stirring constantly, until bubbly; remove from heat. Stir in wine and chicken broth. Heat to boiling, stirring constantly. Boil and stir 1 minute. Stir in bacon.

Heat water (1½ to 2 inches) to boiling; reduce to simmer. Break each egg into measuring cup or saucer; holding cup close to water's surface, slip 1 egg at a time into water. Cook until desired doneness, 3 to 5 minutes. Remove eggs with slotted spoon. Place 2 eggs on bottom half of each croissant; spoon wine mixture over eggs. Serve with top half of croissant.

*Eight English muffins, split and toasted, can be substituted for the croissants. Place 1 egg on each muffin half; spoon wine mixture over eggs.

Following pages: Holiday Braid, upper middle (page 94), Sherried Eggs with Asparagus, left, Italian Sausage Skillet, right (page 88) and Mulled Cider, upper right (page 96)

Ham-Cheese Omelet Roll

$\frac{1}{4}$ *cup margarine or butter*
$\frac{1}{2}$ *cup all-purpose flour*
2 cups milk
4 egg yolks
$\frac{1}{2}$ *teaspoon salt*
Dash of ground red pepper
2 teaspoons snipped chives
4 egg whites
$\frac{1}{4}$ *teaspoon cream of tartar*
$\frac{1}{3}$ *cup grated Parmesan cheese*
Cheese Sauce (right)
$1\frac{1}{2}$ *cups finely chopped fully cooked*
smoked ham
2 tablespoons snipped parsley
$\frac{1}{2}$ *cup milk*

Grease jelly roll pan, $15\frac{1}{2} \times 10\frac{1}{2} \times 1$ inch. Line bottom of pan with waxed paper; grease lightly and flour. Heat margarine over medium heat until melted. Remove from heat; stir in flour. Cook over low heat, stirring constantly, until smooth and bubbly. Remove from heat; stir in 2 cups milk. Heat to boiling, stirring constantly. Boil and stir 1 minute. Remove from heat. Beat in egg yolks, one at a time. Stir in salt, red pepper and chives. Cool at room temperature, stirring occasionally. (Cover mixture to prevent formation of film.)

Heat oven to 350°. Beat egg whites and cream of tartar in large mixer bowl until stiff but not dry. Stir about $\frac{1}{4}$ of the egg whites into egg yolk mixture. Gently fold egg yolk mixture and Parmesan cheese into remaining egg whites. Pour into pan. Bake until puffed and golden brown, about 45 minutes.

While omelet is baking, prepare Cheese Sauce; keep warm. Stir ham and parsley into 1 cup of the sauce. Immediately loosen omelet from edges of pan; invert on cloth-covered rack. Spread omelet with ham mixture; roll up from narrow end. Stir $\frac{1}{2}$ cup milk into remaining sauce; heat. Pour part of sauce over roll; serve remaining sauce separately. Sprinkle roll with snipped parsley, if desired.

CHEESE SAUCE

1 small onion, finely chopped (about
  ¼ cup)
3 tablespoons margarine or butter
3 tablespoons flour
1 teaspoon dry mustard
Dash of pepper
1½ cups milk
1 cup shredded Swiss cheese
5 drops red pepper sauce

Cook and stir onion in margarine in saucepan until onion is tender. Blend in flour, mustard and pepper. Cook over low heat, stirring constantly, until mixture is smooth and bubbly. Stir in milk. Heat to boiling, stirring constantly. Boil and stir 1 minute. Add cheese and pepper sauce; stir until cheese is melted.

Smoked Salmon–Broccoli Soufflé

4 SERVINGS

1 small onion, chopped (about ¼ cup)
¼ cup margarine or butter
¼ cup all-purpose flour
⅛ teaspoon pepper
½ cup milk
½ cup dry white wine
3 eggs, separated
¼ teaspoon cream of tartar
1 package (10 ounces) frozen chopped
  broccoli, thawed and well drained
4 ounces smoked salmon, flaked or
  chopped

Heat oven to 350°. Butter 1-quart soufflé dish or casserole. Cook and stir onion in margarine in 2-quart saucepan over low heat until tender. Stir in flour and pepper. Cook over low heat, stirring constantly, until bubbly; remove from heat. Stir in milk until blended; stir in wine. Heat to boiling, stirring constantly. Boil and stir 1 minute; remove from heat.

Beat egg whites and cream of tartar in medium bowl on high speed until stiff but not dry. Beat egg yolks in small bowl on high speed until very thick and lemon colored, about 3 minutes; stir into wine mixture.

Stir about one-fourth of the beaten egg whites into wine mixture. Fold wine mixture into remaining egg-white mixture. Gently fold in broccoli and salmon.

Carefully pour into soufflé dish. Bake uncovered until knife inserted halfway between center and edge comes out clean, 60 to 65 minutes. Gently divide soufflé into portions, using 2 forks. Serve immediately.

Belgian Waffles

2 eggs
2 cups all-purpose flour
½ cup margarine or butter, melted, or
   vegetable oil
1¾ cups milk
1 tablespoon sugar
4 teaspoons baking powder
½ teaspoon salt
Cardamom Cream, if desired (below)
Sliced strawberries
Blueberries

Heat Belgian waffle iron. Beat eggs in medium bowl with hand beater until fluffy; beat in remaining ingredients except strawberries and blueberries just until smooth. Pour batter from cup or pitcher onto center of hot waffle iron. Bake until steaming stops, 3 to 5 minutes. Remove waffle carefully. Top baked waffle with strawberries and blueberries.

Note: Regular waffle iron can be used; bake times may be slightly shorter.

CARDAMOM CREAM

¾ cup chilled whipping cream
¼ cup packed brown sugar
¼ teaspoon ground cardamom
⅓ cup dairy sour cream

Beat whipping cream, brown sugar and cardamom in chilled small bowl on high speed just until soft peaks form, about 2 minutes. Fold in sour cream.

Breakfast Steaks

1 pound boneless steak (about ¾ inch
   thick)
1 tablespoon vegetable oil

Tenderize boneless bottom or top round steak with unseasoned tenderizer as directed on package. Cut beef into 4 pieces. Heat vegetable oil in 12-inch skillet. Cook beef uncovered over medium heat until brown; turn. Cook until desired doneness, about 10 minutes longer for medium doneness. Sprinkle with salt and pepper.

Chicken and Mushroom Crepes

Crepes (below)
1 cup milk
1 cup chicken broth
1/4 cup all-purpose flour
1/2 teaspoon salt
1/4 teaspoon pepper
1/4 cup margarine or butter
2 cups cut-up cooked chicken
1 1/2 cups sliced fresh mushrooms (about
    4 ounces)
1 jar (2 ounces) pimiento, drained and
    chopped

Prepare Crepes. Mix milk, chicken broth, flour, salt, pepper and margarine in 2-quart saucepan. Heat to boiling over medium heat, stirring constantly. Boil and stir 1 minute. Stir in chicken, mushrooms and pimiento; heat through.

Heat oven to 350°. Spread about 1/4 cup chicken mixture down center of each crepe; roll up. Place seam side down in ungreased oblong pan, 13 × 9 × 2 inches. Pour remaining chicken mixture over crepes. Bake until hot, 15 to 20 minutes.

CREPES

3/4 cup all-purpose flour
1 1/2 teaspoons sugar
1/4 teaspoon baking powder
1/4 teaspoon salt
1 cup milk
1 tablespoon margarine or butter, melted
1/4 teaspoon vanilla
1 egg

Lightly grease 7- or 8-inch skillet; heat until hot. Beat all ingredients with hand beater until smooth. For each crepe, pour 2 tablespoons batter into skillet; rotate skillet until batter covers bottom. Cook until golden brown. Gently loosen edge with metal spatula; turn and cook other side until golden brown. Stack crepes, placing paper towel between them. Keep crepes covered to prevent them from drying out.

Note: Crepes can be made ahead. To refrigerate, stack 6 cooled crepes, placing paper towel between them. Wrap in aluminum foil and refrigerate no longer than 2 days. To freeze, wrap in aluminum foil, label and freeze no longer than 3 months. When ready to use, thaw wrapped crepes at room temperature about 1 hour. To reheat: Heat oven to 350°. Heat wrapped stacks of refrigerated crepes until hot, about 10 minutes, wrapped stacks of frozen crepes about 15 minutes.

Following pages: Chicken and Mushroom Crepes, left, and Melon Salad, right (page 90)

Italian Sausage Skillet

1 pound Italian sausage, cut into 1-inch
slices
1½ teaspoons olive or vegetable oil
2 ounces mushrooms, sliced
½ large red onion, cut into ⅛-inch
slices
½ chopped green bell pepper

Cook sausage in oil in 10-inch skillet over medium heat until brown and no longer pink inside, 20 to 25 minutes. Add mushrooms and onion; reduce heat. Cover and simmer, stirring occasionally, until vegetables are tender, about 10 minutes. Add green pepper. Cover and simmer until green pepper is tender, about 5 minutes.

Apples and Potatoes

4 medium potatoes (about 1½ pounds),
cut into 1-inch cubes (about 4 cups)
2 tart apples, sliced
1 tablespoon sugar
4 slices bacon, cut into 1-inch pieces
1 medium onion, sliced
1 tablespoon margarine or butter,
softened
Dash of ground nutmeg

Heat 1 inch salted water (1 teaspoon salt to 1 cup water) to boiling. Add potatoes, apples and sugar. Heat to boiling; reduce heat. Cover and cook until potatoes are tender, 10 to 15 minutes; drain.

Fry bacon until crisp; drain. Cook and stir onion in bacon fat until tender. Place potatoes and apples in serving bowl. Dot with margarine; sprinkle with nutmeg. Top with onion and bacon.

Bacon Curls

12 slices bacon

Set oven control at broil and/or 550°. Cut 12 bacon slices in half; roll each and secure with wooden picks. Broil 4 to 5 inches from source of heat 2 minutes. Turn; broil 2 minutes longer or until bacon is crisp.

Canadian-style Bacon and Sausage Skillet

4 SERVINGS

*¹/₄ pound Canadian-style bacon, cut into
   ¹/₈-inch slices*
*1 package (8 ounces) brown-and-serve
   sausage links*
¹/₄ cup maple-flavored syrup
¹/₈ teaspoon ground cloves

Place bacon in cold 12-inch skillet. Cook over low heat, turning bacon to brown evenly on both sides, 8 to 10 minutes. Remove from skillet; keep warm. Cook sausages in same skillet as directed on package; drain. Add bacon and syrup. Sprinkle with cloves. Cook, stirring constantly, until sausages and bacon are coated, 2 minutes.

Apple-Grapefruit Salad

8 SERVINGS

4 unpared apples, sliced
3 grapefruits, pared and sectioned
Salad greens
Pomegranate seeds
Lime-Honey Dressing (below)

Arrange apple slices and grapefruit sections on salad greens; sprinkle each serving with pomegranate seeds. Serve with Lime-Honey Dressing.

LIME-HONEY DRESSING

*3 tablespoons frozen limeade or lemonade
   concentrate, thawed*
3 tablespoons honey
3 tablespoons vegetable oil
¹/₄ teaspoon poppy seed

Shake all ingredients in tightly covered jar; refrigerate.

Melon Salad

2 cups watermelon balls
2 mangoes or papayas, pared and sliced
1/2 honeydew melon, pared, seeded and
    thinly sliced
3/4 cup seedless red grape halves
1 large bunch watercress
Citrus Dressing (below)

Arrange fruits on watercress. Drizzle with Citrus Dressing.

CITRUS DRESSING

1/3 cup vegetable oil
1/4 teaspoon grated lime peel
2 tablespoons lime juice
1 tablespoon honey

Shake all ingredients in tightly covered container.

Fruit Platter

3 oranges, pared and cut into slices
2 grapefruit, pared and sectioned
2 kiwifruit, pared and sliced
1 jar (16 ounces) stewed prunes, drained
1 bag (8 ounces) figs
Lettuce leaves

Arrange fruit on lettuce leaves. Cover and refrigerate up to 3 hours.

Dried Fruit Compote

1 package (8 ounce size) mixed dried
    fruit
1/2 cup dried figs
1 1/2 cups water
1/4 cup raisins
1 tablespoon honey
1 teaspoon lemon juice

Cut dried fruit and figs into bite-size pieces. Heat dried fruit, figs, water and raisins to boiling; reduce heat. Cover and simmer until tender, about 20 minutes. Stir in honey and lemon juice. Top with sweetened whipped cream and sliced almonds, if desired.

Easy Valentine Strudels

½ cup margarine or butter, softened
2 cups all-purpose flour
½ teaspoon salt
1 cup sour cream
Cherry-Chocolate Filling (below)
3 tablespoons margarine or butter, melted
Pink Glaze (below)

Cut ½ cup margarine into flour and salt with pastry blender. Stir in sour cream until soft dough forms. Wrap and refrigerate at least 2 hours.

Heat oven to 350°. Grease cookie sheet. Prepare Cherry-Chocolate Filling. Divide dough into 3 equal parts; refrigerate 2 parts dough. Roll 1 part dough into rectangle, 15 × 10 inches, on lightly floured cloth-covered board.

Brush 1 tablespoon of the melted margarine lengthwise over about ⅔ of rectangle. Spread ⅓ filling gently over margarine. Roll up tightly, beginning with filling side. Place on cookie sheet, bringing ends together to make heart shape. Repeat with remaining 2 parts dough.

Bake about 40 minutes or until light golden brown. Cool 15 minutes. Drizzle with Pink Glaze.

CHERRY-CHOCOLATE FILLING

1 jar (12 ounces) cherry preserves
¼ cup orange marmalade
2 cups thinly sliced almonds
¼ cup semisweet chocolate chips

Mix all ingredients.

PINK GLAZE

1 cup powdered sugar
1 tablespoon margarine or butter, softened
½ teaspoon almond extract
1 drop red food color
1 to 2 tablespoons milk

Mix powdered sugar, margarine, almond extract, red food color and milk until desired consistency.

Following pages: Easy Valentine Strudels, left, and Smoked Salmon—Broccoli Soufflé, right (page 83)

Holiday Braid

1 package active dry yeast
¼ cup warm water (105° to 115°)
¾ cup lukewarm milk (scalded, then cooled)
¼ cup sugar
¼ cup shortening
1 teaspoon salt
1 egg
½ cup raisins
½ cup chopped almonds
1 teaspoon grated lemon peel
⅛ teaspoon ground mace
3½ to 3¾ cups all-purpose flour
1 egg yolk
2 tablespoons cold water
Powdered Sugar Glaze (below)

Dissolve yeast in warm water in large bowl. Stir in milk, sugar, shortening, salt, egg, raisins, almonds, lemon peel, mace and 1¾ cups of the flour. Beat until smooth. Stir in enough remaining flour to make dough easy to handle.

Turn dough onto lightly floured surface; knead until smooth and elastic, about 5 minutes. Place in greased bowl; turn greased side up. Cover; let rise in warm place until double, about 1½ hours. (Dough is ready if indentation remains when touched.)

Punch down dough. Divide into 4 equal parts; roll 3 of the parts into 14-inch strips. Place close together on lightly greased cookie sheet. Braid loosely; pinch ends together and fold under. Divide remaining part into 3 pieces and roll each into 12-inch strip. Braid strips; place on large braid. Cover and let rise until double, 45 to 60 minutes.

Heat oven to 350°. Mix egg yolk and cold water; brush on coffee cake. Bake until golden brown, 30 to 40 minutes. Spread with Powdered Sugar Glaze while warm.

POWDERED SUGAR GLAZE

1 cup powdered sugar
3 to 4 teaspoons water

Mix powdered sugar and water until of spreading consistency.

Basil Butter

½ cup margarine or butter, softened
3 tablespoons snipped fresh basil leaves
2 teaspoons lemon juice
¼ teaspoon salt

Beat all ingredients. Serve with croissants, bagels, English muffins, toast or muffins.

Poppy Seed Bread

2½ cups all-purpose flour
1 cup sugar
¼ cup poppy seed
3½ teaspoons baking powder
1 teaspoon salt
1¼ cups milk
⅓ cup vegetable oil
1 egg
1 teaspoon vanilla

Heat oven to 350°. Grease bottom only of loaf pan, 9 × 5 × 3 inches, or 2 loaf pans, 8½ × 4½ × 2½ inches. Mix all ingredients; beat 30 seconds. Pour into pan(s). Bake until wooden pick inserted in center comes out clean, 9-inch loaf 55 to 65 minutes, 8½-inch loaves 55 to 60 minutes. Cool slightly. Loosen sides of loaf from pan; remove from pan. Cool completely before slicing. To store, wrap and refrigerate no longer than 1 week.

Cappuccino

4 SERVINGS

2 cups milk
1 cinnamon stick
2 cups hot Italian coffee
Ground cinnamon

Heat milk and stick of cinnamon in saucepan until milk comes to a boil. Let simmer 10 minutes. Remove cinnamon stick. Combine equal parts of coffee and milk mixture in a demitasse cup. Sprinkle with ground cinnamon just before serving.

French Café Brûlot

8 SERVINGS

8 measuring cups of extra-strong coffee
6 lumps of sugar
2 one-inch cinnamon sticks
8 dashes powdered cinnamon
8 dashes powdered cloves
2 jiggers brandy
4 clove-studded baked oranges*

Serve in silver bowl with hot baked oranges floating in it. Combine all ingredients except baked oranges for each 8 measuring cups of coffee.

*To bake oranges, place in baking pan with a little water and bake in oven (325°) for 1 hour.

Hot Cranberry Punch

¼ cup packed brown sugar
3½ cups water
½ teaspoon pumpkin pie spice
1 can (16 ounces) jellied cranberry sauce
2 tablespoons lemon juice
1 can (6 ounces) frozen orange juice
concentrate, thawed

Mix brown sugar, 1 cup of the water and the pumpkin pie spice in Dutch oven. Heat to boiling over high heat, stirring constantly. Boil and stir until sugar is dissolved; remove from heat. Stir in cranberry sauce until well blended. Stir in remaining water, the lemon juice and orange juice concentrate. Heat to boiling; reduce heat. Simmer uncovered 5 minutes.

Mulled Cider

1 quart sweet apple cider
½ teaspoon whole cloves
½ teaspoon whole allspice
3-inch stick of cinnamon

Heat all ingredients to boiling; cover and simmer 20 minutes. Strain and serve hot.

Orange-Yogurt Drink

2 cups unsweetened orange juice
1 cup unflavored yogurt
2 teaspoons sugar
½ teaspoon grated orange peel

Place all ingredients in blender container. Cover and blend on high speed 10 seconds.

Banana-Orange Drink

2 bananas
1 cup orange juice
1 cup cold milk
1 pint orange sherbet (2 cups), slightly
softened
Orange sherbet

In a bowl mash peeled ripe bananas with a fork. Stir in orange juice. Beat mixture until smooth with a rotary beater. Stir in milk and ½ pint orange sherbet; beat until smooth. Pour into large glasses. Top each glass with several scoops of orange sherbet. Decorate each glass with an orange slice, if desired.

RED SPOON TIPS

Nutrition News

It's no surprise to learn that breakfast is the most important meal of the day—it's what we have heard for years from parents, teachers and nutrition experts. What is surprising is how we can redefine breakfast in ways that take its nutritional importance into account, while accommodating personal taste, busy schedules, differing body clocks and the need for variety. Whether you wake with the birds and look forward to a hearty breakfast or wake, hear the birds and wish they weren't so loud, breakfast can be a delicious and pleasant experience that enriches the entire day. The information below will help you bone up on the nutritional nuances of breakfast, as well as give you unbeatable breakfast strategies.

- Studies show that children function better in school and solve schoolwork problems more easily if they have not skipped breakfast.

- Studies also show that adults who skip breakfast are more physically and mentally sluggish. One study even found that men and women who ate breakfast lived longer than those who didn't.

- Skipping breakfast can bring on overindulgence through a case of nutritional rationalization, such as "Since I didn't eat breakfast, I can have this midmorning doughnut," or "I can splurge with pecan pie and whipped cream for lunch." Spreading meals and calories throughout the day is a much healthier way to eat.

- A well-rounded breakfast should include carbohydrates (cereal, bread, etc.), protein (milk, cheese, meat, fish, etc.), fruits or vegetables and some fat (butter, peanut butter, etc.).

All-New and Different

When you are racing against the clock before work or school, try some of these simple suggestions for a breakfast that fills your nutrition needs but is kind to your hectic timetable. Remember, as long as you keep your meal nutritionally balanced, you can eat almost anything for a healthful and delicious breakfast—let your imagination run wild!

- What did you have for dinner last night? Heating up leftovers for breakfast can be just the thing for a fast and different meal. Some possibilities: rice and beans with a sprinkling of cheese, tuna noodle casserole, vegetable soup, leftover chicken in pita bread, toasted pound cake with fresh fruit or leftover pizza.

• Sprinkle plain or flavored yogurt with granola, fruit and nuts in any combination that strikes your fancy.

• Make a peanut butter and banana sandwich on toast, or try a peanut butter and apple sandwich.

• Warm a previously baked potato and serve with yogurt and chives.

• Eat dip made with cottage cheese, yogurt or vegetables, and use toasted whole wheat bread and vegetables for dippers.

• Be all-American and eat the breakfast that early settlers learned to love—a big juicy slice of apple pie. Add a wedge of Cheddar cheese for extra protein as well as great taste.

Not Before Noon, Please

Many people think it's impossible to eat before noon and need special coaxing to reap the benefits of eating breakfast. By following these easy tips, even the most entrenched nonbreakfast eaters will become members of the breakfast club.

• Use an automatic coffee maker with a timer and set it to brew 15 minutes before the alarm goes off. The smell of freshly brewed coffee will act as a lure to the kitchen and help to start the day on a pleasant note.

• Don't force children, or adults, to eat immediately in the morning. Allow them to wake up as much as possible before serving breakfast.

• Less is more for slow starters. Serve small portions of food. As breakfast becomes more of a habit, you will be able to serve larger breakfasts.

• Be sure and serve food that appeals to the nonbreakfast eater. For example, if a child absolutely refuses to eat the healthful oatmeal that you think necessary, give up the battle and serve a breakfast that the child finds appealing. You may find that serving favorite foods solves the breakfast problem immediately as some people, whether children or adults, find specific foods unpalatable in the early morning. If you make your own breakfast, remember to give yourself license to eat what you find appealing, not just what you think you ought to eat. A little creativity can solve a lot of eating problems.

• For those people who absolutely can't eat before leaving for work or school, pack a doggie bag. Yogurt with fruit, a sandwich, a blender drink in a thermos, cheese or granola will be welcome at least by mid-morning, if not earlier, and will ensure that the body doesn't fall into a blood sugar slump before lunch.

Breakfast Express

Of course there are lots of people who love breakfast, and their only beef is that they don't have enough time to fix their favorite meals every day. You can refer to the chapter Lazy Day Breakfasts (page 62) when you want a delicious breakfast without a lot of fuss, but there are many tips that can help you have a fast and satisfying breakfast on a weekday, or even a weekend when you have engagements and need to be up and out of the house at an early hour.

Blender drinks are an easy breakfast, and one that can be made almost instantly.

Although they are delicious all year, blender drinks truly come into their own in the summer when fresh fruit is readily available and a cool drink is a refreshing way to start a warm day. Try one—or all—of the blender drinks below.

Spiced Tropical Cooler

1 SERVING

1 container (6 ounces) pineapple yogurt
1 banana, sliced
1 tablespoon frozen (partially thawed) orange juice concentrate
1 tablespoon honey
1 or 2 dashes ground cinnamon
Dash of ground nutmeg

Place all ingredients in blender. Cover and blend on high speed about 20 seconds or until smooth.

Peachy Cream Shake

1 SERVING

½ cup drained canned sliced peaches
1 container (6 ounces) peach yogurt
1 or 2 dashes vanilla
Dash of ground nutmeg

Place all ingredients in blender. Cover and blend on high speed about 10 seconds or until smooth.

Banana Cream Pie Shake

1 SERVING

½ cup vanilla ice cream
1 container (6 ounces) banana custard-texture yogurt
½ banana, sliced
Dash of vanilla

Place all ingredients in blender. Cover and blend on high speed about 10 seconds or until smooth. Top with whipped cream and sprinkle with ground nutmeg, if desired.

Yogurt Crème Brûlée

*3 cups cut-up fresh or canned mixed
fruit*
*2 containers (6 ounces each) strawberry,
raspberry or plain yogurt*
⅓ cup packed brown sugar
2 tablespoons margarine or butter
1 teaspoon water
½ cup slivered almonds, toasted

Divide fruit among 6 serving dishes. Top with yogurt. Heat brown sugar, margarine and water to boiling in 1-quart saucepan over medium heat, stirring constantly. Boil and stir 2 minutes. Pour over yogurt. Let stand 5 minutes. Sprinkle with almonds.

Note: Yogurt can also be used to make a quick Crème Brûlée, elegant enough for any gourmet's breakfast.

Make a breakfast sandwich that you can assemble quickly and eat at home or on the run. Listed below are suggestions for different breads and fillings that will make delicious combinations. Try a biscuit with a sausage patty, a poached egg between toasted English muffins, croissants with sliced chicken or a bagel with sliced salmon, cream cheese and onion. The combinations are almost endless.

BREADS

Rye bread
Pumpernickel bread
Whole wheat bread
French bread
White bread
Pita bread
Nut bread
Raisin bread
Bagels
Croissants
Onion rolls
English muffins
Biscuits

FILLINGS

Fried eggs
Poached eggs
Scrambled eggs
Sliced hard-cooked eggs
Bacon
Canadian-style bacon
Fried sausage patties
Tuna salad
Sliced salmon
Sliced chicken
Sliced turkey
Peanut butter
Cream cheese
Swiss cheese
Monterey Jack cheese
Sliced apples
Sliced bananas
Chopped nuts

MICROWAVE REHEATING DIRECTIONS

MEDIUM (50%) POWER

SERVINGS	ROOM TEMPERATURE	FROZEN
1	15 to 30 seconds	45 seconds to 1¼ minutes
2	25 to 40 seconds	60 seconds to 1½ minutes
3	35 to 60 seconds	1¼ to 1½ minutes
4	45 seconds to 1¼ minutes	1½ to 3 minutes

The microwave can speed up any cooking, and it is particularly helpful when you want a fast breakfast. Use it to reheat or warm frozen biscuits, muffins and coffee cakes, following the tips above.

To reheat biscuits, muffins and coffee cakes, place the amount you are heating on a paper towel or napkin (do not cover) and follow the time and direction chart below. Medium (50%) power is recommended, to avoid overheating. Always check at the minimum time because breads are porous and cook quickly. Overcooking toughens breads and causes fillings, frostings and fruits in breads to get too hot, since fillings heat even more quickly than breads. Breads should be warm, not hot and steamy.

Morning Jump Starts

Another way to save time in the morning is to prepare as much of the meal ahead as possible. Pulling a ready-to-bake bread out of the refrigerator is a boon on a busy morning—see Overnight Cinnamon Rolls (page 76). You'll find that putting in a little prep time in the evening pays off handsomely the next morning.

▪ Set the table the night before, and lay out all serving utensils and dishes so you won't have to scramble in the morning.

▪ Prepare frozen juices in the evening and have them ready to pour in the morning.

▪ Measure as many dry ingredients as possible the night before—flour, sugar, spices, etc.—and cut up ingredients that will keep in the refrigerator overnight, such as onions, celery and carrots.

▪ The night before, remove from the freezer and place in the refrigerator anything that needs to thaw for breakfast.

▪ Choose breakfast entrées that can be made the night before, such as Oven French Toast (page 27); then pop it in the oven in the morning. Prepare a cooked fruit compote, or bake extra potatoes at dinner to be used as a quick entrée the next morning.

▪ Bake muffins, sweet breads and coffee cakes during the weekend, or when you have extra time, and freeze them. Use your microwave to heat them directly from the freezer, or put them in the refrigerator the night before to thaw and in the morning reheat them in the oven.

• Get the whole family involved. While you fry bacon, someone else can make toast and be responsible for placing margarine and jellies on the table, while someone else pours juice and prepares hot beverages.

• Always have dry cereals in the house. Almost nothing beats a bowl of your favorite cereal with fresh milk and topped with luscious, ripe fruit. It's so good, you may want to eat it even on days when you don't have to rush.

Terrific Coffee and Tea Techniques

No time is a well-brewed eye-opener more welcome than at breakfast. Whether you are nonfunctional before the first cup of java hits your system or just enjoy the delicate taste of tea to start the day, you'll benefit from the guidelines below.

About Coffee

• Start with a thoroughly clean coffee maker. Wash after each use with hot, soapy water and rinse well with hot water; never scour with an abrasive pad. When cleaning an automatic coffee maker, follow the manufacturer's directions.

• Always use fresh coffee and freshly drawn cold water. Never use hot water, especially in automatic coffee makers; it changes percolating time.

• Serve steaming-hot coffee as soon as possible after brewing. If coffee must stand any length of time, remove grounds and

hold coffee at serving temperature over very low heat.

• Keep ground coffee tightly covered.

PREPARATION METHODS

Automatic: Follow manufacturer's directions for selecting grind of coffee (special ones are available), measuring and brewing the coffee and holding the coffee at serving temperature.

Drip: Measure cold water and heat to boiling. Preheat coffeepot by rinsing with very hot water. Measure drip-grind coffee into filter paper in cone or into filter section of coffeepot, depending on the type of drip pot used. Pour measured fresh boiling water into upper container; cover. When dripping is completed, remove upper container and filter section.

COFFEE CHART

STRENGTH OF BREW	FOR EACH SERVING*	
	GROUND COFFEE	WATER
Weak	1 level tablespoon	¾ cup
Medium	2 level tablespoons	¾ cup
Strong	3 level tablespoons	¾ cup

*Best general recommendation.

Large Quantity Coffee

Measure regular-grind coffee into a clean cloth sack; fill only half full to allow for expansion of coffee and free circulation of water. (Soak and rinse sack thoroughly before using.) Tie sack, allowing sufficient length of cord for fastening to handle of kettle.

Heat measured amount of cold water to full rolling boil; reduce heat. Tie sack to handle; submerge in water. Keep kettle over low heat. Brew, pushing sack up and down frequently for proper extraction, 6 to 8 minutes. When coffee is done, remove sack, permitting all extract to drain into kettle.

QUANTITY COFFEE CHART

PEOPLE	SERVINGS (⅔ CUP EACH)	GROUND COFFEE	WATER
12	23	2 cups	4 quarts
25	46	4 cups	8 quarts

Note: For 25 people, based on half the people using cream and sugar, you will need 1½ cups cream (1 tablespoon per cup) and ½ cup or 25 cubes sugar (1 teaspoon per cup).

About Tea

The tea you buy is a delicate blend of some 20 to 30 varieties. Quality varies according to the soil, climate and altitude in which it is grown and the age and size of the leaves when they are picked.

Broadly classified, there are three types: black, oolong and green.

Black tea derives its color from a special processing treatment in which the leaves are allowed to oxidize. This turns the leaves black and produces a rich brew.

Oolong tea is semioxidized. Its leaves are brown and green. It brews light in color.

Green tea is not oxidized; thus the leaves remain green. The brew is pale green in color.

PREPARATION METHOD

Whether you use loose tea or tea bags, the preparation method is the same:

▪ Start with a spotlessly clean teapot made of glass, china or earthenware. Add rapidly boiling water; allow to stand a few minutes, then pour out.

▪ Heat cold water to a full rolling boil.

▪ Add tea or bags to the warm pot, allowing 1 teaspoon of loose tear or 1 tea bag for each cup of tea desired. Pour boiling water over tea (¾ cup for each cup of tea); let stand 3 to 5 minutes to bring out the full flavor. Stir the tea once to ensure uniform strength.

▪ Do not judge the strength of tea by its color; you must taste it.

▪ Strain the tea or remove the bags. Serve with sugar and milk or lemon, if desired.

Prepare instant tea, a concentrate, according to the directions on the jar.

Iced Tea

Prepare tea as directed except double the amount of tea. Strain tea over ice in pitcher or into ice-filled glasses.

Note: Tea that has been steeped too long or refrigerated will become cloudy. Pour a small amount of boiling water into tea to make clear again.

Do-Ahead Iced Tea

Use 2 teaspoons loose tea or 2 tea bags for each cup of cold water. Place tea in glass container; add water. Cover and refrigerate at least 24 hours. Serve over crushed ice.

Perfect Eggs

Eggs are the backbone of the American breakfast—whether served sunny-side up with toast and bacon, presented in poached form in an elegant Eggs Benedict, served in charming egg cups for a European touch or scrambled for a crowd. Everyone has a favorite form of eggs, and with the information below you will be able to egg yourself on to the best breakfasts ever.

BUYING EGGS

Eggs are marketed according to size, grade and color. Standards for grade and size of eggs are established by the U.S. Department of Agriculture.

Size: Eggs are most often available as extra large, large and medium. Our recipes were tested with large eggs.

Grade: The quality of both the egg and its shell at the time the egg was packed determines the grade. There is very little difference in quality between Grades AA and A, and there is no difference in nutritive content. Almost no Grade B eggs are sold in the retail market.

Color: Eggshell color—white or brown—and yolk color—pale or deep yellow—vary with the breed and diet of the hen. White eggs are most in demand, but in some parts of the country brown are preferred. Flavor, nutritive value and cooking performance are the same for white and brown eggs.

EGG BASICS

- Purchase eggs from a refrigerated case and refrigerate immediately upon arriving home.

- Look for eggshells that are clean and not cracked. If a shell cracks between the market and home, use the egg as soon as possible in a fully cooked dish.

- Store fresh eggs in their carton to help prevent them from absorbing refrigerator odors.

- Store eggs with the large ends up to help keep the yolk in the center.

- Hard-cooked eggs can be stored in the refrigerator one week. Do not freeze.

- Fresh eggs can be stored in the refrigerator 4 to 5 weeks.

- To measure 1 cup, you need 4 to 6 whole eggs, 8 to 10 whites or 12 to 14 yolks.

Soft-cooked Eggs

Place eggs in saucepan; add enough cold water to come at least 1 inch above eggs. Heat rapidly to boiling; remove from heat. Cover and let stand until desired doneness, 1 to 3 minutes. Immediately cool eggs in cold water several seconds to prevent further cooking. Cut eggs into halves; scoop eggs from shells.

Boiling Water Method: Place eggs in bowl of warm water to prevent shells from cracking. Fill saucepan with enough water to come at least 1 inch above eggs; heat to boiling. Transfer eggs from warm water to boiling water with spoon; remove from heat. Cover and let stand until desired doneness, 6 to 8 minutes. Immediately cool eggs in cold water several seconds to prevent further cooking. Cut eggs into halves; scoop eggs from shells.

Hard-cooked Eggs

Place eggs in saucepan; add enough cold water to come at least 1 inch above eggs. Heat rapidly to boiling; remove from heat. Cover and let stand 22 to 24 minutes. Immediately cool eggs in cold water to prevent further cooking. Tap egg to crackle shell. Roll egg between hands to loosen shell, then peel. Hold egg under running cold water to help ease off shell.

Boiling Water Method: Place eggs in bowl of warm water to prevent shells from cracking. Fill saucepan with enough water to come at least 1 inch above eggs; heat to boiling. Transfer eggs from warm water to boiling water with spoon; reduce heat to below simmering. Cook uncovered 20 minutes. Immediately cool eggs in cold water to prevent further cooking. Tap egg to crackle shell. Roll egg between hands to loosen shell, then peel. Hold egg under running cold water to help ease off shell.

Poached Eggs

Heat water (1½ to 2 inches) to boiling; reduce to simmering. Break each egg into custard cup or saucer; holding cup or saucer close to water's surface, slip 1 egg at a time into water.

Cook until desired doneness, 3 to 5 minutes. Remove eggs from water with slotted spoon. A special egg-poaching pan can be used for very simple poaching. Follow manufacturer's directions.

Fried Eggs

Heat margarine, butter or bacon fat in heavy skillet to ⅛-inch depth just until hot enough to sizzle a drop of water. Break each egg into custard cup or saucer; carefully slip 1 egg at t time into skillet. Immediately reduce heat to low.

Cook, spooning margarine onto eggs, until whites are set and a film forms over yolks (sunny-side up). Or gently turn eggs over when whites are set and cook until desired doneness.

Poached-fried eggs: heat just enough margarine, butter or bacon fat to grease skillet. Cook eggs over low heat until edges turn white. Add ½ teaspoon water for 1 egg, decreasing proportion slightly for each additional egg. Cover and cook until desired doneness.

Scrambled Eggs

For each serving, stir 2 eggs, 2 tablespoons milk or cream, ¼ teaspoon salt and dash of pepper with fork. Stir thoroughly for a uniform yellow, or slightly for steaks of white and yellow.

Heat ½ teaspoon margarine or butter in skillet over medium heat just until hot enough to sizzle a drop of water. Pour egg mixture into skillet.

As mixture begins to set at bottom and side, gently lift cooked portions with spatula so that thin, uncooked portion can flow to bottom. Avoid constant stirring. Cook until eggs are thickened throughout but still moist, 3 to 5 minutes.

Fancy Scrambled Eggs: For each serving, stir in 2 tablespoons of one or more of the following: shredded Cheddar, Monterey Jack or Swiss cheese; chopped mushrooms; snipped chives; snipped parsley; crisply cooked and crumbled bacon;* finely shredded dried beef;* chopped fully cooked smoked ham.*

*Omit salt.

Dare to Eat a Peach, and More

Fruit in the morning is not just a nutritional necessity; it can be a treat as well. While a glass of orange juice is always pleasant, you can be more daring and inventive, even making fruit the star of your breakfast. Bite into a fully ripe and juicy peach for a succulent start to your day, and pair it with yogurt for a complete and satisfying meal. There are almost as many breakfast ideas as there are fruits to choose from, and below you will find some suggestions to perk up your morning fruit.

- Take advantage of fruit in season. Just-ripe cherries, strawberries, blueberries, raspberries or sliced apricots, plums or peaches are delicious over vanilla yogurt.

- Have an Italian breakfast by wrapping prosciutto, an Italian ham, around fresh cantaloupe slices or cubes.

- Broil grapefruit, topped with honey, in the broiler until lightly browned.

- Mound fruit over waffles, pancakes, or leftover unfrosted cake, such as pound cake, sponge or angel food. Top with whipped cream, if desired.

- Make a fruit salad of your favorites—grapes, apples, strawberries and melon, for example, and serve with cottage cheese.

- Eat a cold fruit soup, topped with a dollop of sour cream.

- In winter, serve baked apples or poached pears for morning fruit.

- Set out a fruit-and-cheese plate for an easy, help-yourself breakfast.

- Serve a Waldorf salad to spice up a breakfast entrée.

- Slice a fresh pineapple and serve in the pineapple shell.

- Make a warm fruit compote and serve with slices of ham, chicken or turkey.

- Slice apples and serve with sliced cheese, such as Swiss, Cheddar and Monterey Jack.

Breakfast in Bed

Making someone breakfast in bed is a true act of generosity, and it can be just the thing to make a person feel pampered and special. In England, it is common for a thoughtful host to bring guests tea in the morning while they are still in bed. Try this with your next guest—or your spouse—and you'll be surprised how such a small action can have such a large impact. Breakfast in bed is a wonderful way to kick off a birthday, Mother's or Father's Day, an anniversary, a long weekend or just to relax and enjoy the start of the day.

• Use a bed tray with legs to make eating easier—many basic trays are surprisingly inexpensive. If a bed tray isn't available, use a large tray that can be easily balanced on the diner's lap.

• Be sure there are plenty of pillows to prop behind the diner for back support and comfort.

• Place a fresh flower on the tray to brighten the meal.

• Avoid very tall stemmed and lightweight glasses as they tip easily.

• Make the meal easy to eat—serve softened butter and spreads for breads; put jelly on toast directly, rather than serving in the jar, and cut melon wedges into pieces. This will make breakfast in bed a pleasure, rather than a balancing act.

• Include the morning paper on the breakfast tray.

• Provide plenty of napkins in case of spills or dribbles.

Best Bets for Calorie Counters

Many people are watching their weight and want to cut calories across the board. Breakfast is an especially easy meal to make healthful as well as low in calories. Focus on fruits, or eggs that are boiled, poached or scrambled without fat, or yogurt and cottage cheese. In general, if you avoid foods fried in fats, sugary pastries and cereals, and large servings of hard cheeses, you can assemble a very filling and nutritious breakfast that is well within reasonable calorie limits. A bowl of cereal—without a sugar coating—is an excellent breakfast when you add fruit and substitute skim milk for whole milk.

Remember when counting calories that portion control is very important. Two ounces of hard cheese melted on a split English muffin is a good breakfast choice, whereas six ounces of cheese melted on two split English muffins will exceed your low-calorie goals. Below is a list of recipes that are good choices for lower-calorie breakfasts.

Cantaloupe Salads

Chocolate-laced Kiwifruit with Orange
   Sauce

Harvest Celebration Cups

Scrambled Eggs with Peppers and
   Tomatoes

Honey Strawberries

Easy Fruit Salad

Southwest Smoothie

Mulled Cider

Orange-Yogurt Drink

Apple-Grapefruit Salad

Oven Scrambled Eggs

Eggs with Wine Sauce

Fruit Platter

Melon Salad

Banana-Orange Drink

Spicy Peach Salad

Easy Popover Pancake

Pretty Fruit Salad

Fruit-Cheese Kabobs with Ginger Dip

Quick Chili-Cheese Puff

Broiled Honey Grapefruit

Baked Bananas

Fruit in Honeydew Shells

Eggs with Broccoli

Minted Cottage Cheese Salad with Fruit

Mimosa

Smoky Beef and Cheese Quiche

Salt-rimmed Tomato Juice

Fresh Fruit Frappé

Menus

When you want to plan special breakfasts, the menus below can give you some excellent ideas.

BREAKFAST IN BED

Bagels with Lox, Cream Cheese and Onion

Chocolate-laced Kiwifruit with Orange Sauce (page 16)

Mimosa (page 59)

Coffee and milk

FAMILY BREAKFAST

Crisp Waffles (page 22)

Mixed Berry Syrup (page 35)

Bacon

Strawberries and sliced starfruit

Milk

VALENTINE'S DAY BREAKFAST

Champagne

Smoked Salmon–Broccoli Soufflé (page 83)

Assorted Berries

Easy Valentine Strudels (page 91)

Milk

Cappuccino (page 95)

LAZY DAY BREAKFAST

Oven Omelet (page 62)

Canadian-style Bacon

Spicy Peach Salad (page 72)

Toast

Banana-Orange Drink (page 96)

Coffee

Milk

BREAKFAST FOR A CROWD

Texas Breakfast Tacos (page 45)

Southwest Guacamole (page 57)

Fresh Tomato Salsa (page 57)

Festival Eggs (page 42)

Refried Black Beans (page 57)

Sliced papaya

Fiesta Hot Chocolate (page 60)

INDEX

Senior Vice-President and Publisher: Nina Hoffman
Senior Editor: Rebecca W. Atwater
Editor: Anne Ficklen
Assistant Editor: Rachel Simon
Photographer: Anthony Johnson
Food Stylist: Paul Grimes
Prop Stylist: Sharland Blanchard
Art Directors: Patricia Fabricant, Frederick J. Latasa
Production Manager: Lessley Davis
Assistant Managing Editor: Kimberly A. Ebert